THE CATSKILLS
in the ICE AGE

THE CATSKILLS

in the

ICE AGE

by Robert Titus

PURPLE MOUNTAIN PRESS
Fleischmanns, New York

First Edition
1996

Published by
PURPLE MOUNTAIN PRESS, LTD.
Main Street, PO Box E3
Fleischmanns, New York 12430

Copyright © 1996 by Robert Titus

Library of Congress Cataloging-in-Publication Data

Titus, Robert, 1946–
    The Catskills in the ice age / by Robert Titus. — 1st ed.
        p.   cm.
    Included bibliographical references.
    ISBN 0-995796-77-0 (pbk. : alk. paper)
        1. Glacial epoch—New York (State) Catskill Mountains.
    2. Glacial landforms—New York (State)—Catskill Mountains.
    I. Title.
    QE697.T57   1996
    551.7 ' 92 ' 0974738—dc20   96–20441
                                                                    CIP

Manufactured in the United States of America
Printed on acid-free paper

Cover design: Jerry Novesky

Contents

	Foreword	3
1	Reading Landscapes	5
2	The Glaciers of Middleburgh	9
3	The Great Advance	14
4	The Illinoian Glaciation	20
5	The Glaciers of Olana	24
6	Dance Floors	28
7	An Island in a Sea of Ice	35
8	Wild Rocks I Have Known	40
9	Ice Margins	45
10	The Spillways of Olive	48
11	The Notches	52
12	The Glaciers of Overlook Mountain	55
13	The Glaciers of West Kill	59
14	The Glaciers of North Lake	64
15	The Glaciers of Kaaterskill Clove	68
16	The Glaciers of East Kill	71
17	The Glaciers of Windham	74
18	The Halls of the Schoharie	77
19	The Glaciers of Grand Gorge	82
20	Glacial Lake Grand Gorge	86
21	The View from Vromans Nose	90
22	Retreat in the West	95
23	Retreat Along the Susquehanna	102
24	The Glaciers of Council Rock	106
25	The Upper Susquehanna Lake Chain	110
26	Drumlins Along the Mohawk	115
27	The Legacy	119
	Important References	122

Foreword

This book is not a definitive scientific treatise on Catskill glaciers, but an introduction for the general reader. Read it indoors if you must. In fact, it would be a good idea to read through it once before the outdoor season. But this book is meant to be stuffed into a backpack or a glove compartment and carried to where the glaciers once were.

Geology is an outdoor science, and that is where it ought to be enjoyed. Bring this book to the top of Slide Mountain and read Chapter 7. Carry it to the edge of the cliff at Vromans Nose and read Chapter 21. Travel along the Susquehanna and read Chapter 23. In short, go and see what the glaciers have done here in the Catskills.

While preparing this book, I received help and encouragement from a number of people. My thanks to Dr. Sam Adams, Doris West Brooks, Suzanne Dudley, Dr. Jay Fleisher, Sharon French, and Dr. Michael Kudish.

Advancing and retreating glaciers leave the landscape a mess and destroy most evidence of what had been there. That's why I occasionally use fantasy in describing some scenes in the book. It is written as plausibly as possible, but not meant to be taken too seriously.

1

Reading Landscapes

THERE IS PROBABLY no natural wonder more universal than the night sky. As daylight dims and twilight approaches, the stars and the planets come into view, one by one. On a moonless night, away from urban lights, the growing darkness brings into view a spectacle that people have been pondering ever since our species first evolved. The view is that of the universe itself, and all of us gaze at it, in awe of its size, its depth, and its mysteries. We often do this while we are alone. It makes us feel that we are, individually, very small, but at the same time part of something very big.

Nobody actually needs to know very much about the night sky in order to appreciate this natural wonder, but there is a big difference between just *looking* and actually *seeing* what is there. Recognition leads to understanding, and understanding is what makes observing nature truly rewarding.

Like all geologists, I have spent many nights outdoors. I have passed much of that time gazing at the sky, and I have come to know the sights fairly well. There are hosts of well-known and obscure stars that are often grouped into the constellations. There are planets that soon become recognizable by their brightness and color. Then there is the Milky Way, our "from-the-inside" view of the very galaxy we inhabit.

There is only one steady beacon in the night sky: Polaris, the North Star, which never moves, at least from our perspective. The rest of this great nighttime panorama is dynamic, and its image is constantly changing. All the other stars move, passing above, east to west, as the night progresses. And they move with the seasons. As the new year dawns, the constellation Orion, the hunter, dominates the late night sky; within it is the bright "red giant," Betelgeuse. Later in the season, the stars forming Leo, the lion, become the beacons of late winter. I am always glad to see the return of Arcturus, the herald of spring. With late spring, the Milky Way rotates to form a glowing ring that rims the entire horizon. Summer brings its own constellations; chief among these are Scorpio, the scorpion, and its companion, the archer Sagittarius. In mid-summer, the Milky Way rises above the horizon and looms as a great disc of stars, arcing overhead. Late summer brings meteor showers, and soon thereafter the first nighttime harbinger of fall—the late-night appearance of Pegasus, with its great square of stars. Near Pegasus is Andromeda, our nearby sister galaxy. They are soon joined by the seven sisters of the Pleiades. Finally, as the yearly cycle comes to an end, the greatest of all the stars—Sirius—rises, twinkling white, green and red above the winter horizon.

This view of eternity, however, may not always be there. Air pollution has already robbed many millions of people of the best of this view and, in many urban centers, light pollution has already made the universe all but invisible. How would you feel if the nighttime sky was slowly (or quickly!) disappearing into a haze of industrial smog? The answer is obvious: The public outcry would be enormous.

But what if you had *never* seen a starry night sky? There are any number of natural atmospheric compositions that might have blocked our view of these wonders. If our atmosphere had been only a little bit more humid, for example, we would hardly be able to see the stars at all. Then our reaction to that hypothetical deprivation would be different, for we don't miss something we don't even know about. Consequently, there would be very little outrage.

And that is the point. This book is not about stars; it is about perception. It's not about the universe, but about the landscape around us. There is so much that we can see around us if we develop a trained eye.

Like any geologist, I have become perceptive to the stories my eyes have learned to read from the rocks and landscapes that are always around me. This is one of the great pleasures of my science. Sometimes bedrock speaks of ancient oceans and sea floors inhabited by exotic-looking creatures. In the rocks I can see the comings and goings of those oceans of the past. Other stratigraphic sequences tell me of the rise and fall of whole mountain ranges that no longer exist. I am, for example, fond of exploring the Acadian Mountains of New England, even though those peaks have not existed for 300 million years or more.

There are riveting moments to be seen in the past. I once came across a mass kill of trilobites, those exotic arthropods of the Paleozoic, on a freshly exposed slab of rock. What a marvel it was to see the jumble of skeletons lying on one large slab of rock. I still wonder what happened on one awful day so long ago to kill all those poor creatures.

My specialty is paleontology, and most of my work involves the study of ancient fossil organisms. Most of the stories I could tell are about ancient marine creatures. Nevertheless, I believe that nothing in my experience as a geologist has been more illuminating, or has affected me more, than learning to see the many features that have been left upon our Catskill landscapes by recent glaciations. Not that long ago, a sheet of ice a half mile or more thick overwhelmed and buried these mountains. The advance and eventual melting of that huge mass of ice dramatically affected the region. I cannot travel anywhere in the Catskills without being confronted with the evidence of glaciation—and I mean a *lot* of evidence, clearly and easily read from the landscape.

There is in the Catskills the image of a natural wonder, nearly as impressive as the night sky: our picturesque mountains, once as completely buried by ice as is Greenland today. But, like the night sky, we have to learn how to *see* this wonder. This book is about seeing landscape in a new way, with a trained eye. It is about reading landscape. It's not difficult or time-consuming. In fact, it's a great deal of fun, and the rewards are many.

One thing is certain: You will find that you did not understand Catskill landscapes until you learn what the glaciers have done here.

2
The Glaciers of Middleburgh

COUNTY ROUTE 36, the small road that heads south from Middleburgh, in Schoharie County, parallels the Schoharie Creek. It runs upon the river's eastern flood plain for about two miles, then gently rises about 250 feet. At various locations on that incline, you can turn and view Middleburgh, and the whole of the northern Schoharie Creek Valley. The flood plain is broad and flat, and extends off to the north and south.

Across the valley is the steep front of Vromans Nose (figure 2-1). That small hill would be of no particular significance except

2-1. Vromans Nose from Route 145.

for the shear cliff that makes up its south-facing front. This impressive feature enhances its apparent elevation and has earned it the name "sky island of the Schoharie." Vromans Nose also has a steep east-facing slope, as does the next mountain to the north. The two east-facing slopes are lined up to make a nearly single wall (figure 2-2) split by Line Creek. It is an impressive landscape feature which shows up better on a map.

The eastern side of the valley matches the western side. Here again, steep slopes tower above Middleburgh. It's a curious landscape, its flat valley floor and the steep "walls" rising above, and it gives the impression of a hallway of stone.

Twenty three thousand years ago, the view from this location was very different from what it is today. The most surprising difference was that the valley floor was probably not flat. Instead,

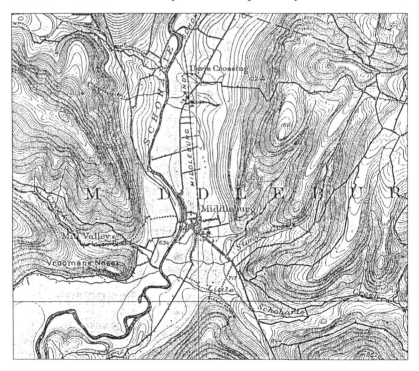

2-2. Schoharie Creek, Middleburgh.

the valley walls sloped gently toward a Schoharie Creek that was at a lower elevation than it is today. All was forest then, from the river banks to the top of the highest hills. There is no telling exactly what the composition of that forest was—a mixture of softwoods and hardwoods, hemlocks, beach, chestnuts and oaks seems reasonable. The forests abutted the shady, moss-covered banks of the stream. The riverbed varied considerably from place to place, with bouldery whitewater stretches and deeper, quieter pools. Stream ecology varied similarly, and there were many different species of plants, birds, fish and insects to be found.

The seasons came and went, as they do today, but the climate was changing. Had people been there to record changes, they might not, even over a lifetime, have noticed any; climate shifts are subtle. The oak, hemlock and beeches were doing poorly. The very old and young trees were dying. The winters weren't that much colder than those we experience today, though there was a great deal of snow. But the summers were noticeably different—it just did not warm up until late in the season, and gradually the growing seasons shortened. The trend continued primarily in one direction—toward cooler summers and snowier winters (Dawson, 1992).

Decades passed, and then centuries, and still the climate did not warm. Instead, the effects of the climatic cooling accelerated at an alarming rate. One by one, local species dwindled and disappeared; whole species were driven from the region. Now there were winters so severe that trees were killed—a few at first, then many. Soon, dense stands of gray, bare tree trunks ruled the upper slopes near Middleburgh, while the lower slopes maintained only an unhealthy and pale greenery. Then the lower slopes also joined the forest of the dead. The soils became permanently frozen, and this sealed the fate of those last few remaining trees that had hung on.

Trees do not make noise, but with their death the forests, once loud with a cacophony of insect, bird and animal life, fell silent. The trees could not leave, but animals could, and their populations had slowly migrated away to better climes. The only noise was from the occasional falling of dead limbs.

The weather continued to get worse, reflecting a fundamental change in the climate. Now cold conditions persisted all year round, and it was common for strong prevailing winds to blow out of the northeast for days at a time. The winds made a mess of the brittle old trees.

Then there must have been a summer when the snow did not all melt. The old drifts of dirty snow in the shaded glens were covered by a fresh white in early September. Soon there was another such summer, and then another. And, with time, there were a lot of such "summers." Snow piled up in annual strata around the trunks of the dead trees of the dead forest. Schoharie Creek became permanently frozen, so none of the precipitation could drain from the valley. Snow began to pile up so much that the valley started to fill with it. The still-standing dead trees disappeared beneath the white.

Eventually, something new appeared at the northern end of the valley. At first, it must have looked like a low-lying bank of clouds, like fog in the valley. It did not move, but remained ominously stationary on the horizon. The whiteness swelled taller, and with time it was clear that it was drawing closer. During the mid-day hours, its surface gleamed bright white in the sun. In late-afternoon shadows, it darkened, and its yellow top graded down to a greenish-blue front. Eventually the advancing white wall began to fill the valley. A knowledgeable person would have recognized it as a great glacier by then, but there were no people here to see this sight.

As the glacier continued south, it loomed higher and higher. As it approached Middleburgh, the sharp details of its fractured and broken front became clearer. The ice was being pushed from the north by the hundreds of miles of massive glacier that lay behind it. As vectors of energy competed to push it forward, the badly strained ice creaked, cracked and groaned. Here and there, some masses of ice were thrust ahead of others.

Soon the white wall stretched across the entire northern horizon in what would have been a frightening image. But while the whole glacier was heading south, it was the ice of the valley that led the way. By now, an observer would be forced to retreat away from the advancing ice, perhaps down the valley to the village of Fultonham. There, with eyes fixed on the advancing valley ice, it must have been a shock when another mass of ice appeared on the mountain above, tumbling over edge of the steep slope there.

The glacier was enormous, and the region was being overwhelmed. Behind its leading edge, the glacier was at least 3,000 feet thick, a plateau of ice that spread across all of the northern horizon. The valley ice plowed right through the region. With its final approach came the muffled sound of whole stands of brittle, buried tree trunks being snapped off and bulldozed away. Middleburgh was of no importance to this glacier; it did not pause in its advance, but instead continued on down the valley and off to the south. Soon the whole upper Schoharie drainage basin lay entombed beneath the thick ice. Then all of the Catskills disappeared beneath the advancing glacier.

3

The Great Advance

O VER THE PAST two million years, several cycles of glaciation have swept across North America. The one which had the greatest effect upon the Catskills as we know them was the most recent one, the *Wisconsin glaciation*. That event ended only about 12,000 years ago, and it is the main focus of our story.

At their maximum, the Wisconsin glaciers covered most of Canada and the northern United States (figure 3-1). They formed over three different geographic centers: the *Keewatin center*, in western Canada, the *Labrador center*, and the *Greenland center*.

The Greenland center is still much as it was at the peak of glaciation. The other two have long been inactive, but tens of thousands of years ago they were great centers of snow accumulation. The Keewatin center had no influence upon the Catskills; our glaciers came from Labrador. Ice sheets advanced from there and reached as far south as Cape Cod and Long Island. To the west, the advance stretched across northern New Jersey, Pennsylvania, and into the Mississippi Valley.

The processes which initiate glaciations are beyond the scope of this book, but the direct cause of this glaciation was simple: The climate changed. The winters did not actually get that much colder, though they were very snowy; the summers changed the

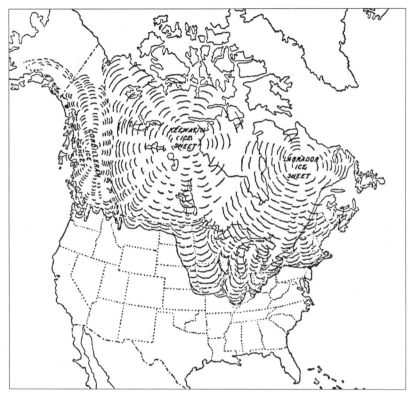

3-1. Wisconsin glaciers of North America.
(Chamberlain and Sallisbury, 1927)

most—they became colder (Dawson, 1992). Under these circumstances it snowed a lot in Canada. Year after year, abundant winter snowfall was followed by cool summers which did not melt all of the snow, so there was a net annual accumulation.

Deep snow, as it piles up, compacts and hardens into the brittle material we know as ice. When the ice gets thick enough it becomes plastic and begins to move as a very sluggish fluid, especially if there is a slope. Much of the movement is accomplished as ice crystals slowly slide past each other. Also, the whole mass of ice may slide across a thin sheet of meltwater. (That's the way an ice skater glides along—on thin films of water beneath his skate blades.) All of this is most effective at temperatures near the freezing point. That's warm for a glacier, and it is warm glaciers that move the quickest (Flint, 1971).

About 25,000 years ago, the snow and ice began to thicken considerably in Labrador. The ice became plastic as its thickness increased, and it spread out from its thick center of accumulation. When a glacier gets large enough, it becomes what glaciologists call an *ice sheet*; this one has come to be called the *Laurentide Ice Sheet*. The flow was away from the center of maximum thickness, toward its thin periphery. That gave the glacier two different realms: a thick interior grading to a much thinner periphery. This is important because the two realms behave entirely differently as the glacier advances across surrounding countryside.

The behavior of an ice sheet is affected by the underlying landscape. Where the landscape was relatively flat, such as in the midwest, the ice sheet tended to advance easily, and its thin front expanded into very large semicircular lobes (see figure 4-2). That seems to have been the case as the Laurentide Ice Sheet moved southward from its Labrador center; there were few landscape features to block the flow of ice in Quebec.

The landscapes of New York State and New England are different, however. Quite a few mountains interfered with and deflected the flow of ice. East and west of the Adirondacks, though, there were some "alleys" that allowed the flow of ice, and glacial lobes took advantage of these. Several of these lobes (two large, two smaller) affected New York State (figure 3-2). The first of the large lobes, the *Ontario Lobe*, advanced toward the Catskills out of Ontario, from the northwest, but it stopped short of the our region. The other large lobe was the *Hudson-Champlain Lobe*, which advanced through the Champlain lowlands, down the Hudson Valley, and then southwest across the Catskills. This lobe was the one that advanced farthest south, reaching Long Island and northern New Jersey. The two smaller lobes were the *Adirondack Lobe* and the *Mohawk Lobe*, which laid between the two larger masses of ice.

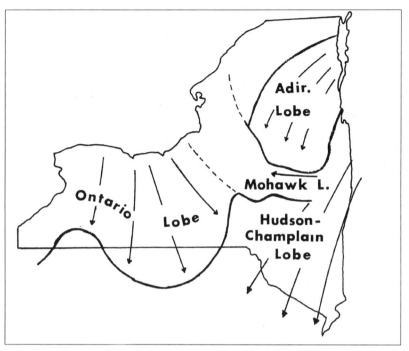

3-2. The lobes of ice of New York State.
(Isachsen, et. al., 1991)

The only lobe of real importance in the Catskills was the Hudson-Champlain Lobe. It advanced down the Champlain lowland; as it approached the Catskills the flow split, much of it continuing south through the lower Hudson Valley, while some of it was deflected westward into the Mohawk Valley, becoming the Mohawk Lobe. The rest of the ice made the assault upon the Helderberg Mountains and entered the Catskills.

But the advancing ice was hardly affected by the Helderbergs. Remember, while the periphery of a glacier is quite thin, the interior of the ice sheet is very much thicker—in this case thicker than the Helderbergs were tall. The thin front of the Hudson-Champlain Lobe was being pushed from behind by a very large mass of ice. Thus, the ice was almost always flowing downhill, away from its Labrador center, even as it was crossing the front of a mountain range. In short, a mountain 1,200 feet tall could not stop a glacier 3,000 feet thick.

Beyond the Helderbergs, the Catskills were more effective barriers to the flow of ice. Although they couldn't stop the flow, they did influence the thin leading ice. The landscapes of the eastern and northern boundaries of these mountains were steep, elevated, and varied. There was the steep Wall of Manitou on the east, and to the north of it, the Northeastern Escarpment. Both had major gaps. The leading edge of the advancing ice sheet exploited these gaps in the mountain range: The ice entered and flooded those valleys. I have already described the flow of ice down the Schoharie Creek Valley to Middleburgh. Other early local advances probably occurred down the Susquehanna River, into Kaaterskill and Plattekill cloves, and up the valley of Esopus Creek. But these penetrations of the Catskills were just the advance guard of the ice.

The Laurentide Ice Sheet thickened as it advanced, and the local variations in landscape had much less influence on its flow. Eventually, the greatest thickness of the ice overrode all of the Catskills and then continued south. It was as if a great tide of water had risen and overwhelmed the Catskills. The ice over the Catskills advanced into northern New Jersey, while the ice in the Hudson Valley continued to Long Island (see figure 4-1).

There is a limit to the advance of even great glaciers, however. Generally, glaciers do not advance beyond about 40 degrees north of the equator, because it simply stays too hot south of that line. The Laurentide Ice Sheet was no exception—it advanced into New Jersey and reached a line extending from Cape Cod to Long Island, but it could go no farther. New ice was being fed from the Labrador center, far to the north, and that ice actually continued to advance to the south, but along its southern front the advance was balanced by an equal amount of melting. When an advance of ice is balanced by its melting, the stalemate is called a *glacial still-stand*.

Along the front of ice at a still-stand, great masses of gravelly sediment accumulate. These materials are carried to the front of the glacier by the advancing ice. Ice and sediment reach the front; the ice melts and the sediment is left behind (see figure 22-1). These accumulations are called *terminal moraines*. A big glaciation produces a big moraine; the Wisconsin glacier terminal moraine created much of Long Island and Cape Cod.

For a time, an enormous ice cap covered most of North America; our continent lay beneath a mile or so of ice. The magnitude of this event easily compares with present Antarctica or Greenland. This was truly the age of the glaciers, the *ice age*.

4

The Illinoian Glaciation

THE TERMINAL MORAINE of the Wisconsin glaciation is quite a striking landscape feature. It is so big that, even where it has been flooded at Long Island and on Cape Cod, the sea has been unable to submerge it. At Cape Cod, especially, we find that there are actually two moraines: one that makes up the east-west part of the Cape, and another moraine, farther south and more submerged, that makes up Nantucket and Martha's Vineyard. The glacier reached its southernmost line of advance at the site of the islands (the sea floor was then dry land), hesitated at a still-stand, retreated, and then deposited a second

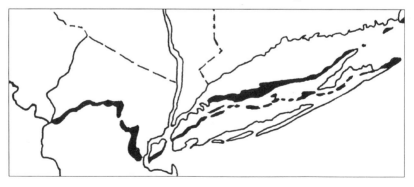

4-1. Moraines of Long Island and New Jersey.

moraine at the Cape during a second still-stand. The first is a terminal moraine; the second is a *recessional moraine.*

The two moraines can be traced west to Long Island, but they merge and form a single moraine through the western half of the island and across northern New Jersey (figure 4-1). If you know what to look for there, it forms an obvious landscape feature. You can see the moraine quite clearly where it is cut by side roads along Route 46 in western New Jersey. The moraine consists of great, hummocky heaps of coarse sand, gravel and boulders. When I was a student at Rutgers, the professors took us to see it. It made quite an impression on me. For the first time, I could envision the great glacier, towering in my mind's eye above the moraine.

The moraine continues westward into Pennsylvania, where the glacier was slowed by the Appalachians, and where its moraine is harder to trace. Beyond are the flat landscapes of the midwest and great plains, where the glacier advanced as unimpeded lobes, reaching well down into Ohio, Indiana, Illinois and Missouri. Farther to the west, the glaciers of the Keewatin center had limited success in penetrating the complexities of the mountains of the Cordillera (see figure 3-1).

The great terminal moraine of the Wisconsin glaciation represents this glaciation at its zenith. This stage of glaciation is called the *Woodfordian advance*; its peak is dated at about 21,750 years ago. The Woodfordian advance is important because it created almost all of the glacial features found within the Catskills.

The terminal moraine is an easily recognized landscape feature all along the southern front of the Woodfordian advance. Being relatively young by geological standards, it always has a fresh, new appearance—there has been little time for erosion. Soils are thin and poorly developed. Easily weathered minerals, such as calcite, are commonly seen in the moraine. Since such minerals dissolve easily, they don't normally survive very long, and so are proof of a moraine's young age.

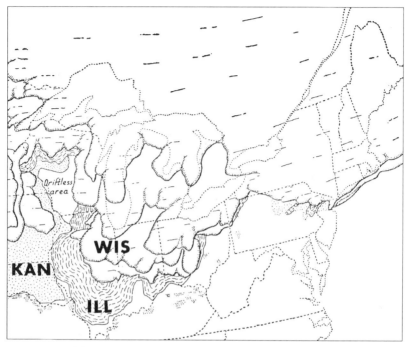

4-2. Wisconsin, Illinoian, Nebraskan, Kansan glaciers.
(Atwood, 1940)

But, as the glacial geologists mapped the Wisconsin glaciations they came to realize that there was another, older glaciation, the deposits of which are found farther south of the Wisconsin terminal moraine. These glacial deposits are more extensively weathered, more deeply eroded, their soils thicker, and are thus much older. The deposits of this glaciation are most extensive in Illinois, and hence were named *Illinoian glaciation*. Similarly, even older glaciations came to be recognized. They have been named the *Kansan*, and oldest of all, the *Nebraskan glaciation* (figure 4-2). The Illinoian ended about 130,000 years ago; the Nebraskan may go back 1.5 million years.

The remains of old glaciations are often difficult to study because they are so deteriorated that much of their original composition and structure have been lost. Where younger glaciations have bulldozed across older ones, the evidence of the older events is generally lost entirely. In the Catskills, the Wisconsin glaciation almost entirely destroyed the remains of the earlier glaciations. Because of this, there is little that can be said about those events. In fact, the evidence is so slim that it is an open question how much the earlier glaciations affected the Catskills.

But not all evidence of these earlier glaciations is gone, and some of our most impressive Catskill landscapes seem to reflect the effects of those earlier glaciers. If there was an Illinoian glacier in New York State, then it is most likely to have flowed down the Hudson Valley. If so, it must have had at least something to do with the carving of that most impressive Catskill feature: the *Catskill Front*, commonly called the *Wall of Manitou*. It was once thought that the long straight wall of the Catskill Front had been scraped into the Catskills by the passing Illinoian ice of the Hudson Valley. The Illinoian event might have some relationship to the two great clefts of the wall—Kaaterskill and Plattekill Cloves. Both display evidence that they were penetrated by Woodfordian ice, but it appears that they were not there until *after* the Illinoian event. Did the Illinoian exert some triggering effect which began the erosion of these cloves? It might be; we don't know. It's a difficult issue.

5

The Glaciers of Olana

Our Catskill landscapes are blessed with a beauty that was described as "sublime" by artists who worked here during the mid-nineteenth century, and glaciers are responsible for a lot of that scenery. Much of the ruggedness of Kaaterskill Clove is the direct result of Woodfordian glaciers moving up that great canyon. Both Haines and Kaaterskill Falls were produced by post-glacial erosion. The basins of both North and South Lakes were scoured out by the passage of ice. And so on. The Catskills appear as they do today because of the Wisconsin glaciation.

Thomas Cole visited the newly opened Catskill Mountain House in 1825 and set about sketching in the vicinity. It was on the Wall of Manitou's great, steep escarpment that he conceived his first important canvases. Those early Catskill landscape paintings established him as an artist, and his success and influence soon grew until he was a very important man in the history of American art. Cole would be acclaimed as a founder of the famed Hudson River School of art. However, it was Frederic Church, Cole's only student, who was to become recognized as the foremost painter of the "school." The Wall of Manitou would also greatly influence Church's life, especially in the year 1867.

5-1. The view from Olana.

For Frederic Church, 1867 was a watershed year (Kelly, 1990). It was, in many ways, a gloomy end to the first half of his life. That youthful half had seen enormous success for Church, who had become the leading figure of American landscape art. He had done a long series of great works which had won him fame and fortune; he was renowned and respected all over the world. And he had become the husband of a beautiful young wife, Isabel. But by 1867 he developed the first stages of rheumatoid arthritis, a disease that would cripple his hands and eventually bring his career as a painter to an end.

In 1867 Church bought land across the Hudson River from the town of Catskill. It was a place he knew very well. Thomas Cole, as Church's teacher, had first brought him there in 1845, and the young Church did some of his first landscape sketches there. The site had a magnificent view of the Hudson River Valley, the Catskills, and the Shawangunk Mountains beyond (figure 5-1). It's a view that had affected the life of Church, and the memory of it is what brought him back to the site in the 1860s.

Frederic and Isabel were beginning a new family to replace their two children lost to diphtheria in 1865; already there was a

5-2. Olana.

baby son, and two more offspring would soon follow. Church would build his home, Olana (figure 5-2), as a Persian revival mansion to house this family. Olana would become the art of the second half of his life. And indeed it was; Church would work on Olana for more than thirty years.

The southwestern view from Olana is a wonder. Below, the Hudson flows wide and flat. Beyond are the lowlands of the Hudson Valley itself. The valley here is wide, but in the distance it is abruptly terminated by the steeply rising Catskill Mountains. The Northeastern Escarpment stretches off to the north; to the south is the Wall of Manitou. The mountains' front is broken by a great cleft—Kaaterskill Clove. Near the clove, with a spyglass Church could have seen the great white Catskill Mountain House, by then the premier resort hotel of the nineteenth century. Indeed, from there, guests of the hotel could, and did, see Olana.

Before his hands became fully crippled, Church painted this view several times, including at least one winter scene. That he would paint a winter scene is not surprising; Church had long been intrigued by Arctic scenery, and he painted a number of polar landscapes, including *The Icebergs* and *Aurora Borealis*. But Church was not a geologist, and it is doubtful that he would have been able to imagine the grand view that could have been seen from the site of Olana more than 130,000 years earlier. That's ironic, as those times were so important in shaping both the Wall of Manitou and his own life as well.

September 23, 135,892 BC, late afternoon

It is a typical September afternoon in this, the time of the Illinoian glaciation. An enormous high pressure system blankets all of the land north of the Catskills, all the way to the North Pole and beyond to Scandinavia. Strong, steady winds are being driven out of the northeast, and are headed toward the future Olana site and on toward the Catskill Front. From there, the winds are blowing up the front of the range. Earlier in the day, none of this could be seen, as the blowing snow obscured the view in all directions. But now, in late afternoon, the winds are at last abating.

The blue of the sky is beginning to break through the snow, and soon, as the wind continues to abate, more of the landscape appears. In the dry Arctic air, the view is perfectly clear: To the southwest are the peaks of the Catskills. Snow banks abut the mountains like an apron of white. Nevertheless, quite a bit of bedrock towers above the deep snow. The mountains are bare rock, and there is no hint of brown soil or green foliage. The lower levels of rocks are brick red; this grades upward into strata of light buff color. The winds generate wispy currents of snow, which are still blowing upward across the visible rock. Gusts of snow rise and fall like foamy waves breaking upon the "shores" of the Catskill Front.

Below and to the south, the slopes of snow grade downward onto a great valley glacier. The entire Hudson Valley is filled with ice. On the right side of this vista, the northern half of the glacier is white, deeply blanketed in last winter's accumulation of snow. Farther south, the fresh snow thins and old ice is exposed; its rough, dirty surface displays crevasses, great fissures that are mostly curved to the south. These numerous crevasses are lined up, closely spaced and parallel to each other. They are dark blue-black, while the ice between them is brilliant white with a thin, recent snow cover. The ice has fractured this way because the mid-valley portions of the glacier have been advancing more quickly than the adjacent ice, dragging upon the slopes of the Hudson Valley. The crevasses give the appearance of motion to the glacier, but the movement is much too slow to be perceived. To the south, the crevasses widen and deepen. Here a lot of melting has occurred during the brief "summer."

To the southwest, the glacier abuts the steep Catskill Front. Here, the moving ice is grinding down and steepening the wall of rock. This is an icy machine of erosion that is carving and sculpting the finishing touches of the escarpment. Southward from the Wall, ice flows are pigmented with a wide stripe of reddish brown. One familiar feature of the scene is missing: While there is a break between High Point and South Mountain, there is no Kaaterskill Clove. The great chasm has not yet been cut into the Wall of Manitou. It will have to wait until after the Illinoian glaciers are gone from the valley.

6

The Dance Floors

ONE OF THE OVERWHELMING things about the study of the Wisconsin glaciation is the vividness of the imprints left upon the landscape by the passage of its advancing glaciers. Few things are more impressive than the *dance floors*, a phrase not found in any of the lexicons of geology. It is a folk term, local to the Catskills. It describes a flat exposure of rock, polished and striated by the sand and rocks carried by a passing glacier. The term was first used to describe the great ledge of Vromans Nose, which towers above the lower valley of Schoharie Creek (figure 6-1).

Vromans Nose is not unique, nor is it the only polished ledge of rock that attracts visitors in the Catskills. Another example is Inspiration Point, in Kaaterskill Clove. At this location the view is of Haines Falls to the west and the Hudson Valley to the east. There is another dance floor on the small ledge atop Pratt Rock on Route 23, just east of Prattsville (figure 6-2). This site can be reached by hiking up the slope to the Pratt carvings, and then continuing up to the right and around the cliff. This ledge is not nearly as well polished as the other two, but it does offer a nice view of the middle Schoharie Creek Valley.

What these three sites have in common are the finely polished and striated surfaces, and the shear cliffs dropping off below.

6-1. The Dance Floor at Vromans Nose.

6-2. The Dance Floor at Pratt Rock.

Such peculiar features have to have a special origin, and that origin is, of course, glacial. Glaciers are dirty—they pick up and carry large amounts of sediment as they move across the landscape. The sediment is varied; it includes clay, silt, sand, gravel, cobbles and boulders. The sediment was swept up by the passing ice and is, of course, concentrated at the base of the glacier. The enormous pressure of a thick glacier presses down upon the sediment, and this scours the underlying bedrock. Over time this exerts a "sanding" effect upon that bedrock, and the rock becomes polished. That's what created the dance floors at Vromans Nose, Inspiration Point and Pratt Rock.

But even a casual observer will notice that there is a lot more than polish on the surface of a dance floor. The final stages in a glaciation leave imprints upon the surface (figure 6-3). The most common is the glacial *striation*, a long, straight, very narrow gouge etched into the rock by the passage of one of the last boulders or cobbles carried across the area by an advancing glacier. These are abundant, as many rocks were likely to have been moved by the passing ice. If a particularly large and broadly concave gouge is found, it is called a *glacial groove*. Striations grade upward into grooves; there is no clear break.

Striations are easy to spot, and they are quite common in any glaciated region. They offer an amateur geologist an opportunity to do some basic research. Armed with a compass and a topographic map, a geologist can search for and record the directions of the ancient flows of the local glaciers. Each site that yields striations is recorded as a compass-direction arrow on the map. As the data accumulate, a graphic view of the flow of the glacier is likely to emerge. (That's how the arrows of figures 3-2 and 18-2 were drawn.) One word of caution, however: Low-elevation striations record the flow of ice funneled by the local landscape; mountain-top striations must be studied to get a regional picture of the movement of an ice sheet (see Chapter 12).

Glacial flow tends to vary over long periods of time. It is not unusual to find several sets of striations in one area, or even on a

6-3. Striations/crescents, two directions.

single dance floor. Older, worn-down striations may align in one compass direction while younger, fresher striations align in another. Different striations in an area are often the best records we have of the complex history of the passage of different glaciers during separate episodes of glaciation. They are a graphic testimony to the fact that glaciations are complex events.

But which way did the glacier go? A compass direction alignment is not a complete answer to that question. Logic tells us that most glacial flow is north-to-south, but this is not without exception. For example, east-and-west alignment of striations is not unusual in the Catskills, and when that is the case it is not immediately clear which way the glacier was moving.

There are things to look for on a dance floor which may help determine the direction of flow. *Crescentic marks*, often called *chattermarks*, are the most interesting. A boulder or cobble, being dragged across bedrock, can produce a variety of crescent-shaped gouges (figure 6-3). Apparently these were formed when

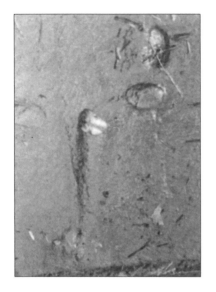

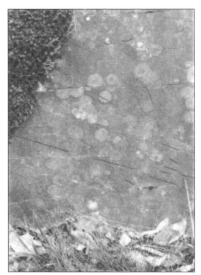

6-4. "Rat Tail"   6-5. Vertical dance floor

the rock "skipped" along under the glacier. They are composed of two fractures from which rock has been chipped away. The gouge is usually thought to be a lot steeper on the downstream side. The "horns" of the crescents can be oriented concave downstream or upstream.

Another feature to look for is a *rat tail* (figure 6-4). It formed when a dense, resistant bedrock cobble stood in the way of the advancing glacier. The cobble was not easily eroded, and it sheltered the sandstone downstream from it. This stretched out rat tail points in the direction of flow. These are not uncommon, but you have to develop an eye for them.

There are vertical dance floors as well. These are relatively uncommon. They form when glaciers rub up against pre-existing cliffs. Once again, the glaciers sand and polish the bedrock, but this time the result is a smooth vertical surface, which often displays striations just as a horizontal dance floor does. Such striations rise in the direction of flow (figure 6-5).

A dance floor is a remarkable glacial landscape feature, but

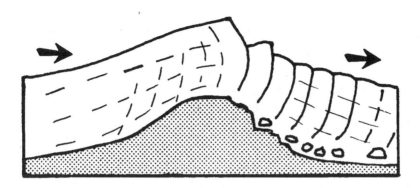

6-6. Scour and pluck topography.

there is also another striking feature: the cliff. Shear cliffs are found associated with a lot of dance floors. One of the best is Vromans Nose, but the cliff at Inspiration Point also is a fine one. Virtually all of the park at Pratt Rock is cliff. There should be some sort of causal relationship between the dance floor and the cliff, and there is. As the glacier moves across a hill, it yanks the bedrock. If the rock is already fractured, great blocks of it will be plucked loose and dragged off by the ice. Over time, the continuing process of *glacial quarrying* or *plucking* will create a steep or even vertical cliff. This type of natural quarrying will continue until the end of glaciation (figure 6-6).

Like striations, these cliffs can be studied to determine the direction of glacier flow. A compass point direction, at a 90-degree angle to the front of the cliff, can be drawn on a map. Along with the striation directions, these markers will document the flow of glaciers. Plucked cliffs at Kaaterskill Clove are common along the trail that hugs the edge of the north slope of the clove. All of these cliffs, including the one at Inspiration Point, face west. They record the westward motion of a glacier moving up the clove. In the Schoharie Creek Valley, a number of cliffs record the motion of glaciers. The cliff at Vromans Nose and the one at Pratt Rock show movement down the valley, as do other cliffs just west of Prattsville and east of Middleburgh.

Scouring and plucking can produce a grain to the landscape. Large, south-facing slopes of the Catskills tend to have been steepened by plucking. Conversely, scouring tends to have sculpted and lowered the north-facing slopes which, therefore, have a much gentler slope. The best example of this can be seen in the view of Vromans Nose from Route 145, east of Middleburgh (see figure 2-1).

7

An Island in a Sea of Ice

IF THE GLACIALLY-SCULPTED Catskills influenced artists, then they certainly affected the writers of the region. John Burroughs, the pre-eminent New York State natural history writer, is closely associated with the Catskills, where he was born and raised. Burroughs certainly knew his way around the Catskills, and he wrote extensively about their natural history, but the one mountain he is most linked to is Slide.

Burroughs first wrote about Slide Mountain when he described his hike to its top in "The Heart of the Southern Catskills." He is honored by an historical marker at the base of the mountain, and by a memorial plaque at its summit. Slide Mountain, and adjacent Cornell and Wittenberg Mountains, make up the "Burroughs Range" of the Catskills.

At 4,180 feet, Slide offers the loftiest climb in the Catskills (figure 7-1). Today it's a favorite goal for many hikers. The rewards of "conquering" Slide are many. Most people focus on the several excellent vantage points—east are Cornell and Wittenberg Mountains, with the Ashokan Reservoir below; northeast is Plateau, Indian Head and Overlook Mountains; to the north is Panther Mountain. If you climb Slide, you can investigate for yourself one of the interesting problems of Catskill glaciations: Did the Wisconsin glaciation cover all of the Catskills, or did one or more of the mountains remain poking through the ice? A peak, sticking through a continental glacier, is called a *nunatak*. Had Slide been a nunatak—an island in a sea of ice—or had it been submerged by the great glacier of about 22,000 years ago? The question is not a very critical one; no important theories hang in the balance. But geologists wonder such things.

In 1916, when John Lyon Rich, a glacial geologist, was surveying Slide, he noted that the slopes of the mountain were clearly scoured by glaciers (Rich, 1935). That was no surprise. We have seen that all of the Catskills show the effects of passing glaciers. They have been scraped, gouged and generally ground up by the passing ice; their soils are thin and only poorly developed. But that was not entirely the case with Slide Mountain: At 3,900 feet, the mountain's landscape changed. Above that level, Rich noticed the ledges of rock were less sharply defined; their corners, once sharp fractures, seemed to have been softened by long ages of chemical weathering. The bedrock ledges were often deeply stained with the yellow and red of iron oxides, a weathering phenomenon he hadn't found in the lower elevations. Loose boulders were rounded, and they displayed iron-stained, weathering rinds. This type of weathering should have taken a lot of time. Rich believed that the high elevation soils were thicker than those below; they were certainly richer in quartz pebbles and quartz sand, which could have been derived only from the extensive, long-term weathering of local bedrock. Rich deduced that the upper 300 feet of Slide Mountain had escaped the grip of the glacier that otherwise had engulfed the rest of the peak, and perhaps all the rest of the Catskills. In short, he concluded, the soils and bedrock at this high elevation were extensively weathered because they had remained there undisturbed for a very long time, high above any passing glaciers.

A differing point of view developed in 1928 when an observation tower was constructed at the summit of Slide. Excavations for the tower's foundation uncovered glacial striations in freshly

7-1. The view from the top of Slide Mountain.

exposed bedrock. George Halcott Chadwick, who devoted his entire career to the study of Catskill geology, was the first to notice these. He immediately concluded that the mountain had indeed been covered with ice. The Wisconsin glacier had buried the tallest peak of the Catskills. How deeply Chadwick did not know, but the glacier must have been enormous.

Rich was not convinced, however. He argued that the Slide Mountain striations must be dated to an older episode of glaciation—he stuck to his view that Slide had been a nunatak during the most recent glaciation.

And that's where the debate ended. Scientific juries don't render verdicts, and nobody was declared the winner. There is, however, a consensus among most of today's glacial geologists to accept Chadwick's argument. Nevertheless, John Lyon Rich was an experienced glacial geologist, and his views cannot be easily dismissed. I decided to see for myself.

On my climb up Slide, the first thing I noticed was that there were indeed changes toward the top of the mountain: Quartz pebbles and quartz sand are very prominent on the trails there; I also found no iron stains until nearly the 3,900-foot level. But what about those striations? I knew where the observation tower had been—a bit of its foundation remains—but I could not find the striations. I am sure they were there in 1928; Chadwick was too fine a geologist to have made a mistake about that, but today they seem to be gone. My only guess is that the striations had been so softened by weathering that they have disintegrated since 1928. They may have dated back to an earlier glaciation, as Rich thought. If so, they would be among those few evidences of a pre-Woodfordian glaciation in the Catskills.

The top of Slide Mountain does match Rich's descriptions, and *does* seem older than the rest of its slopes. Hard answers, however, are difficult to come by in this science. One thing is beyond dispute, though. Slide Mountain records the Laurentide Ice Sheet at its peak. Once, the great ice sheet was lapping the mountain's upper slopes. Meanwhile, the rest of the glacier was expanding all the way south to Long Island and northern New Jersey. It's quite a scene to imagine.

October 14, 20,055 BC, predawn

The night is moonless, and the eastern horizon is still completely dark. The sky is clear, and the stars display themselves with an unusual clarity. They have an intense, icy twinkle to them. The surroundings cannot be seen very clearly yet. The nearby surface is smooth, and it reflects the starlight with a silvery sheen of surprising brilliance. It is quiet, and the predawn atmosphere is almost completely still. But the stillness is broken by a few soft sounds emanating from a short distance to the north. They are intermittent, and while some have a deep muffled sound to them, others are sharp snapping noises, echoing across the darkness.

Now, just before the sun's light begins to appear, there is a breeze. It is gentle, but it gradually picks up. It slowly, methodically swells, and builds, and intensifies into a steady wind from the northeast. A very slight glow gradually appears in the far southeast. It hugs the horizon, and it sharply silhouettes the darkness below. The light is soon bright, and the eastern horizon has broadened; its glow now dominates the vista. All stars, except the brightest, have disappeared. The sunlit horizon is a bright tangerine blur, lying between a thin gray ground fog below and the blue gray sky above. Wind-driven snowflakes blow against the jagged and barren mass of sandstone that makes up the foreground.

As the sun continues to rise, the winds die down again. The snow settles and the great Arctic landscape which, on this day, is the Catskills, emerges from the white. The landscape nearby can now be seen as a large mass of sandstone, mantled in a gravelly soil. Its light color forms little contrast to the surrounding ice. The sandstone rises a few hundred feet above the ice. It is stepped, with sedimentary layers making each of the "stairs." The steps lead up to the small summit very near to the northern edge of this "island." There are a lot of very weathered tree stumps, but these relics of a recent past do little to relieve the barrenness of the scene.

Just over the edge, beyond the summit, a large jumble of broken ice abuts this island of rock. The great sheet of ice is actively advancing out of the north, and its flow is breaking against the rocky impediment—that's where most of the noise has been coming from. The current of ice splits around the rock and flows along the eastern and western slopes. Each current carries with it the dirty plume of sediment it has scraped off the knob of rock.

To the east, other currents of ice are breaking against the unseen summit of Cornell Mountain. This peak is lower—it does not rise above the ice—but there is plume of dirty brown ice to mark its location. A little east of north, other broken masses of ice can be seen in the far distance. More streamers of dirty ice trail away to the south. These mark the locations of the taller ledges of Panther Mountain. The rest of the horizon is bleak, a seemingly endless plateau of ice.

The sun rises higher and the day brightens. The peak of Slide is not entirely bare; there are some pockets of snow. And surprisingly, some of this snow is bright red. Just a few weeks earlier these red patches were a dirty green. The color is from snow-dwelling algae; red is the color of its winter resting phase. The color is appropriate. It is, after all, autumn in the Catskills.

8

Wild Rocks I Have Known

MY FIRST JOB was as a paperboy, delivering the *Paterson Evening News* on Doremus Avenue in Glen Rock, New Jersey. My paper route took me past the biggest rock I had ever seen (figure 8-1). It was, in fact, the rock for which the town was named. The great rock of the glen was an enormous boulder of granite. It was so big that it posed a real problem when the road was paved. Crews cleared away the earth around the rock, and then they paved the road so that the two lanes of Doremus Avenue split—each lane curved around one side of the boulder. Big rocks like this can affect people. Residents of Glen Rock have had a lot of pride in their rock; long ago, they put up a flag pole in front of it and upon it a bronze plaque honoring the war dead.

The bedrock under Glen Rock is all red sandstone; there is no granite native to the area, nor is there any for many miles around. This boulder simply does not match the local geology. In fact, you have to search quite a distance to find any bedrock that matches the Glen Rock boulder. That is why this rock, and many other such petrologic misfits, is called an *erratic*.

Erratics are extremely common, and many of them are so large that they catch a lot of attention. They were first recog-

8-1. The rock at Glen Rock.

nized in Europe back in the early-nineteenth century. At that time these peculiar rocks posed a lot of serious questions. Early-nineteenth-century geologists had not the slightest inkling of glaciations, and they puzzled over how such great boulders could have been transported long distances from where they must have originated. The best solution they came up with was that, during Noah's flood, icebergs bearing the boulders drifted out of the Arctic. As these bergs melted, the boulders dropped out of them and fell upon what was then the sea floor. After Noah's flood was over, these geologists concluded, the boulders were left high and dry. (Today we do see such rocks in icebergs drifting out from Greenland. When these bergs melt and the boulders fall to the sea floor we call them *dropstones*.)

As theories go, this one left much to be desired. It became obvious that many such boulders did not come out of the Arctic, but instead (like the one at Glen Rock) from a relatively short distance to the north. Then too, there were *so many* of them, too numerous, it seemed, to blame on icebergs. Erratics were a real problem for geologists for quite some time.

With the advent of glacial theory, the problem was quickly solved, and it became obvious that the erratics were transported by great continental glaciers. The great Glen Rock boulder had been brought to Doremus Avenue by a lobe of ice that had traveled down the Hudson Valley. It had been plucked loose by that glacier, dragged to New Jersey, and left there during melting.

Not all erratics travel as far; most are transported only short distances. Many of them are small, but the large ones do catch our attention and are important landmarks in a glaciated landscape. In the Catskills, many erratics are well known and have been given names. North Lake State Park is the best place to see some fine erratics. The most picturesque of these, Sunset Rock (figure 8-2), is a boulder left stranded at the top of the great outcrop that overlooks North and South Lakes, the whole southern length of the Wall of Manitou and much of the Hudson Valley beyond. This view began attracting landscape artists in the early-nineteenth century, and many of very fine canvases were done here.

Certainly the most comical of the erratics is Alligator Rock (figure 8-3). This one can be seen along the trail that goes east into the forest from the point which separates North and South

8-2. Sunset Rock.

42

8-3. Alligator Rock.   **8-4. Boulder Rock.**

Lakes. Long after being left where it is today, the lower half of the rock broke loose and fell, making up the gaping lower jaw of the "alligator." (Few people have ever been able to resist putting cobbles into the alligator's mouth to make teeth and then posing for silly pictures.) The woods north of Alligator Rock also are particularly rich in erratics, large and small.

There are several large erratics perched on the edge of the escarpment that easily can be visited. One lies immediately south of the Catskill Mountain House site; another is Boulder Rock (figure 8-4), to the south.

Erratics used to be common along the escarpment, but many of them are long gone. Alf Evers, in his history of the Catskills, recorded what happened to them: They fell victims to a sport called "boulder rolling." It seems that wherever nature left a boulder small enough to be moved, and near the escarpment cliff, it was doomed to be shoved over the edge. Most boulders fell to that fate long ago; the only ones still around are much too large for even several big men to move.

43

Outside of the park at North Lake are a large number of erratics. One of the best known is Devil's Tombstone, at the state park at Stony Clove. Its resemblance to an old bluestone tombstone led to its being hoisted into a standing position (figure 8-5).

The most literary of the Catskill erratics is Boyhood Rock, near John Burroughs' home in Roxbury. This sandstone erratic is found in the pasture above the house where Burroughs grew up. The view from the rock is an especially bucolic Catskill landscape of forested mountains and pastoral valleys. Burroughs knew what an erratic was, and he gained great inspiration from sitting on the rock. Boyhood Rock is a wonderful place to sit any time of the day, anytime of the year. Burroughs is still there: He chose to be buried at this site.

Some of the strangest erratics are *pedestal rocks*, which are seen only occasionally. They are large boulders balanced on three or more smaller ones. As the glacier melted, the large boulder was lowered down upon the smaller ones. There is a good example on the blue trail below North Mountain (figure 8-6).

8-5. Devil's tombstone.

8-6. Pedestal rocks.

9
Ice Margins

THE WOODFORDIAN ADVANCE reached a peak about 21,750 years ago, and it seems to have been followed by a period of glacial stability that lasted for several thousand years. Then, sometime before 18,500 years ago, the ice began a prolonged retreat.

Glacial retreats are complex affairs. Naturally, the event is caused largely by a warming climate, but there are also complex astronomical cycles that alter the seasons. When summers are long and very warm, glaciers melt quickly; when the summers are short and cool, melting slows down. Through complex temperature and seasonal cycles, the climate trends toward an overall moderation.

The so-called retreat of a great ice sheet is not a quick or easy affair. A glacier "retreats" when ice along its front melts. The front does not actually *move* backward—it can't. We say that its front *melts backward*, because that is what happens.

Long periods of warm conditions and long summers promote the retreat of the ice, but these can be punctuated by times of cold which can slow the retreat to a *still-stand*, or even cause a *readvance*. A glacier literally can take two steps backward and one step forward.

Some still-stands are very important events. When a glacier's front is stable long enough, it produces a substantial complex of landscape features called an *ice margin*. Chief among these is the recessional moraine. (One of these is evident on Long Island.) There were several such ice margins in the history of Catskill glaciations. Think of them as the "one step forward" lines.

When recessional ice margins are of sufficient importance we give them names. The oldest ice margin occurred about 17,200 years ago. Commonly named the *Wagon Wheel ice margin*, its active ice advanced down the Hudson Valley, and some of it turned into the lower Esopus Creek (see figure 10-1). A lot more ice flowed actively across the northeastern Catskills as far as the Central Escarpment, creating an ice margin that extended off to the northwest from Esopus Creek (figure 9-1) (Cadwell, 1986). The Wagon Wheel event was followed by a time of melting and retreat all along the front.

The second major ice margin was the *Grand Gorge ice margin* (called the *Rosendale ice margin* in the Hudson Valley) of a little more than 16,000 years ago. The ice retreated from the Wagon Wheel ice margin, and it seems to have melted off all of the higher Northeastern Escarpment peaks. Then there seems to have been at least some readvance. There was a two-pronged attack upon the Catskills. First, ice rose up against the Northeastern Escarpment and penetrated a number of gaps in the Wall of Manitou, including Kaaterskill Clove and the lower end of Esopus Creek. Second, a great deal of ice flowed down the Schoharie Creek Valley. These two masses of active ice combined to create a complex ice margin (see figure 18-2).

Later, the ice retreated from the Catskill Front, and in the Schoharie Creek Valley the ice retreated to a new still-stand at North Blenheim, resulting in the *North Blenheim ice margin* (see figure 20-1). After that, there was a general retreat of ice into the far northern Schoharie Creek Valley. A final ice margin formed during the *Middleburgh readvance* (see figure 21-2) about 15,500 years ago, at which time ice actively advanced

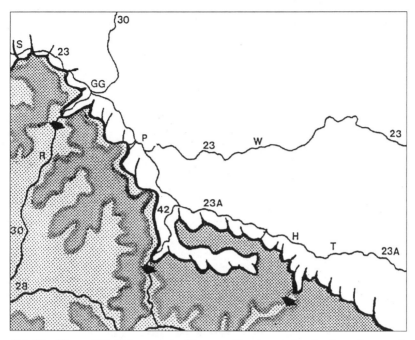

9-1. The Wagon Wheel ice margin. Fingers of ice (arrows) poke through several gaps in the central escarpment. Major highways are marked. Grand Gorge, Windham, Hunter and Tannersville are marked by letters.

down the Schoharie Creek Valley to Middleburgh.

Each of these steps is important, as understanding the regional effects of Catskill glaciation is closely related to the ice margins. Erosion by the glaciers of the ice margins probably destroyed many of the features caused by the earlier glaciations; in effect, that wiped the board clean and left a new record of glaciation. Much of the following discussion about Catskill glaciation is based on the effects of these ice margins.

10

The Spillways of Olive

My INTEREST IN CATSKILLS GLACIERS began in the town of Olive, in Ulster County, where there is a group called The Olive Natural Heritage Association. The group organized in order to investigate the various facets of the natural history within the town. Dr. Morton (Sam) Adams called me and asked if I would survey the geology of Olive, and I agreed to do it.

Funded by a grant from the O'Connor Foundation, which is active in the Catskills, Dr. Adams has assembled a group of botanists, archeologists, entomologists, and one geologist, to tackle the many interesting projects. He has outfitted a small old barn as a pretty decent research lab. The last time I was there, the place was loaded with Cornell biology students who were working on local insects. It's all pretty much "by the seat of the pants," but it is working (Bierhorst, 1995).

The stratigraphy of Olive is pretty straightforward—in fact, not all that exciting. But the *glacial* geology is different. Olive lies just southwest of the Ashokan Reservoir, in the lower reaches of the Esopus Creek Valley (figure 10-1), which faces the Hudson Valley. The town is located near something like the Grand Central Station for the various Wisconsin glaciers, and it's a bit of a struggle to get a handle on all that happened there.

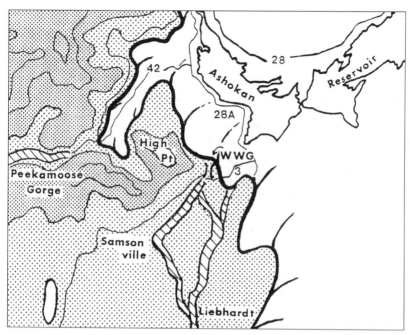

**10-1. Map of the lower Esopus Creek, Wagon Wheel ice margin.
Spillways in diagonals**

The story begins with the Wagon Wheel ice margin. During
that time, an arm of the Hudson Valley glacier advanced up
Esopus Creek. It split into two—one branch of ice penetrated all
the way to Panther Mountain, while the other branch reached
the valley north of High Point (Dineen, 1986). This blocked the
Esopus Creek Valley and impounded water behind an ice dam.
When all of this ice began to melt, the water went in different
directions at different times. Very early, as the glaciation was
peaking, water seems to have been diverted entirely out of the
Esopus Creek drainage basin; it flowed through the gap at the
top of the Bush Kill and, from there, down Rondout Creek,
which quickly became eroded into what is called Peekamoose
Gorge (Rich, 1935).

For a long time, Rondout Creek was a great spillway, draining
all of the water of the Esopus basin. But today, nearly all of that

10-2. Wagon Wheel Gap.

water is gone, leaving a relatively empty gorge with nearly dry waterfalls. The upper Rondout is a typical *underfit stream*—its valley is much larger than such a small stream normally needs (Rich, 1935).

Glacial ice flooded the lower Esopus Valley for the term of the still-stand, but a glacier is not completely stable, even during a stand-still. Its front advances and retreats a bit, and that was probably the case along the Wagon Wheel ice margin: The glacier backed away a little, and abutted against High Point Mountain. Then, in the cleft between the glacier and the mountain, a new spillway opened up. This is the Wagon Wheel Gap (figure 10-2), for which the ice margin is named. It is a deep, narrow gap and dry spillway.

But Wagon Wheel Gap is not all that remains of that rapidly eroded meltwater gorge. For a while, cascades of water carved the Samsonville Gorge while draining off to the south. The small, underfit stream which flows through this gorge today certainly did not carve it. Once again, the landscape speaks of an ancient time when this was a spillway of major proportions.

Later, the Esopus glacier backed away just a little bit more and the Beaver Lake spillway opened up. Again, all we see today is a deep gorge with a small, underfit stream.

During the time of the Grand Gorge ice margin, most of this history was repeated. Glaciers advanced once more into the lower Esopus Valley, but probably not quite as far. Glacial lakes formed in the Esopus Valley and in Maltby Hollow, adjacent to High Point Mountain. At this time, the Beaver Lake spillway was again active.

Today, the best place to see one of these spillways is to approach Samsonville from the northeast on Samsonville Road. The road passes beneath Wagon Wheel Gap and follows one of the old spillways. At Samsonville, there is a good waterfall that dates back to the glacial spillway. Browns Road south becomes De Witt Road, and then crosses another "fossil" waterfall. Sundale Road to Liebhardt leads to Rochester Valley, typical of a very steep and narrow spillway. Sundale Road north or Doug Road south both follow the Rochester Creek spillway.

All of these glacial features—the various spillways, the dry waterfalls and gaps in the mountain—are called *paleo-forms*. They are "fossil" landscape features that date back to when the landscape was being pushed, pulled, gouged and deposited into the shapes you can see today—if you know how to "read" them.

11

The Notches

THE WAGON WHEEL ICE MARGIN was a major event in the glacial history of the Catskills, and it produced several of the most striking landscape features found in our mountains—the notches of the Central Escarpment. The margin formed about 17,200 years ago, when the Laurentide Ice Sheet stabilized along a front extending along the Central Escarpment.

Wagon Wheel Gap is a good feature after which to name this ice margin, because it is typical of the landforms that were produced along the margin. It is an eye-catching landscape feature. More than 200 feet deep and quite narrow, it looks a lot like a wagon wheel rut carved into soft bedrock—the person who named it may have been familiar with such ruts carved by covered wagons on the old Oregon Trail.

Wagon Wheel Gap is a glacial spillway, formed by torrents of meltwater cascaded off of the melting Wagon Wheel ice margin. This was a common event in the Ice Age Catskills, and played a similar role elsewhere in the mountains.

There are three major gaps in the Central Escarpment: Stony Clove Notch in the east, and Deep Notch and Grand Gorge Gap to the west (see figure 9-1, arrows). The lower slopes of each of the notches are quite deep and steep-walled; they speak of ero-

11-1. The Stony Clove Gap.   **11-2. Deep Clove.**

sion by active whitewater streams. Like Wagon Wheel Gap, however, they have virtually no flowing water within them today. They are, of course, very good examples of paleo-forms (figures 11-1, 11-2).

At the time of the Wagon Wheel ice margin, some ice advanced through the three gaps, but for the most part the glacier lapped up against the Central Escarpment and stalled there until the climate warmed, a little less than 17,000 years ago. When the Wagon Wheel ice began to melt, enormous amounts of meltwater had to drain off somewhere. In the west, water flowed easily down the West Branch of the Delaware River. Elsewhere, water backed up between the melting ice and the slopes of the Central Escarpment. Water levels rose until they reached the notches, then poured through them.

Notches are common in the Central Escarpment. Some good examples are Mink Hollow Notch, Pecoy Notch, and Diamond Notch. But these are too elevated and too gently sloped to have had much water flowing through them. Surprisingly, it is likely that both Stony Clove and Deep Notch originally resembled these smaller notches, but when meltwater cascaded through them the resulting erosion must have quickly deepened them to produce their present form.

State Route 42 passes through Deep Notch, and County Route 214 passes through Stony Clove, so you can easily visit both of these sites. As you approach from a distance, you first see the gently inclined upper slopes. Then, as you pass through the notch, you see the spectacular lower slopes, rising nearly vertically hundreds of feet above the valley floor. The beds of railroads and highways have leveled the valley floors from the even narrower notches nature had left.

Approaching these notches from the south, you can imagine the torrents that were pushed from behind by the enormous weight of large reservoirs of water. The powerful currents were squeezed at the base of the notches and the compressed strength of the flow helped the erosion. South of the gaps, the flow fanned out into chattering cataracts of whitewater.

The spillways at Olive and the notches along the Central Escarpment are the major landscape features of the Wagon Wheel ice margin. The next event, the Grand Gorge ice margin, was not the biggest phase of Catskill glaciation, but it was the most recent of the important episodes. Most of the rest of this book is about the features of the Grand Gorge ice margin.

12

The Glaciers of
Overlook Mountain

THERE IS SOMETHING SLIGHTLY UNSETTLING about finding an abandoned road in America. That a road, once small and narrow, should grow with time seems normal. But that a road once important should fall into disuse and abandon just does not seem right in a nation that is crisscrossed with interstate highways. Nevertheless, it does happen, and it has happened in the eastern Catskills.

There are at least two examples of long-abandoned highways in the Catskills. One is the old Mink Hollow Road, which crossed the Central Escarpment of the Catskills between Sugarloaf and Plateau Mountains. The road once carried hides to the tanneries on the Schoharie Creek. That industry disappeared from the region long ago, and the road is now enclosed in the Catskill Forest Preserve.

The other lost road is the Overlook Mountain Road, which once extended the length of the Catskill Front from the top of Plattekill Clove south to Overlook Mountain, and from there to Woodstock. This highway once primarily served the needs of the Catskill bluestone industry, and much of the old road is bordered by abandoned quarries. Neither of the two old roads was ever paved, and both are now marked hiking trails.

The Overlook trail was traversed by glaciers long before any human traffic appeared, and it retains the scars of those times. It is an excellent place to view evidence left by the glaciers as they flooded the Hudson Valley and flowed across the Catskill Front.

The best approach to the Overlook trail is from the Platte Clove Road (Route 16) to the north. Here, just before the road descends the mountain into the clove, you can park and hike up the access trail to the main hiking path. The trail immediately crosses a brook near the road, and then ascends the lower slopes of Indian Head Mountain. The trail is part of the original Overlook Road, and erosion (probably from the old wagon traffic) has cut through the thin soils and exposed bedrock for most of the way.

This exposed bedrock displays a nice, polished surface, and is cut by numerous striations. Some of the striations look older than others. The story begins with a worn, secondary set of striations that indicate an earlier episode of southward glacial movement. These older striations were partially erased by the youngest glacial movement. (My guess is that this poorly-preserved set may have formed during the original Woodfordian advance.) Most of the trail's striations date to these younger events. At lower elevations, the striations are oriented roughly northwest (west 30 to 40 degrees north); that's parallel to the orientation of Plattekill Clove. Farther south, as the trail rises to 2,600 feet, the striations shift to a nearly western orientation, which is not parallel to the clove.

A relatively simple history can be read from the younger striations, which may have been left by the Wagon Wheel ice margin. Early, the ice seems to have been funneled into Plattekill Clove—that's when the northwest-oriented striations were formed. Later, the ice of the Hudson Valley thickened until it filled the whole valley. It then gradually overflowed the valley and crept westward across the Catskill Front. The thicker glacier is less influenced by the underlying topography; thus, with time, the striations indicated westward movement. How far westward the ice penetrated is not known.

Farther south along the crest of the escarpment are a number of abandoned bluestone quarries. During the late-nineteenth and early-twentieth centuries this was a very active area for the bluestone industry. (There is quite a geological story recorded in the sedimentary strata of these quarries—but this book is about glaciers.) Continuing south, the trail reaches the turnoff to Echo Lake, where more evidence of glaciation can be found. More west-oriented striations are found at about 2,900 feet.

The trail to Echo Lake, a spur off the Overlook trail, displays much exposed bedrock, also cut with numerous striations. However, here the striations don't point in a particular compass direction—they all point downhill. The trail continues steeply all the way to the lake.

Echo Lake is not very big, but it is surrounded by a great bowl-shaped depression—the feature which gives the lake its name. The lake's only outlet is at the bottom of this depression. The outlet lies at the head of the deeply carved valley of the Saw Kill, which flows on as a tributary of lower Esopus Creek.

The bowl of Echo Lake is known to geomorphologists as a *cirque*, an amphitheater-shaped depression in which a large field of snow collected during glacial times. Within the cirque, the snow compacted into ice, and was organized into an *Alpine glacier*. Here, the ice flowed out of the cirque and carved the upper valley of the Saw Kill as it ground its way down the mountain. Later, after the glacier melted, Echo Lake was left behind in the floor of the old cirque. This is normal; such lakes are called *tarn lakes*. These are typical Alpine features—that is to say these features are most common throughout the Alps of Switzerland and anywhere else where mountains are, or were, extensively glaciated.

South of the Echo Lake basin is the summit of Overlook Mountain. There, at about 3,100 feet, is an old fire tower, and below the base of the tower is more exposed bedrock showing glacial striations. At such high elevations these are likely to have been left by the original Woodfordian advance. They trend southwest, which is the general regional trend for the flow of ice in the Catskills (see figure 3-2).

The geological evidence found on the Overlook trail provides a good introduction to the effects of the Grand Gorge glaciation on the Catskill Front. The front was attacked at various times by glaciers from both the east and the west. From the east, there were times when the Hudson Valley glacier moved south, thickened and rose westward up the walls of the Catskill Front. There also were times when, in the west, Alpine niches were collecting snow and compacting it into ice. The Echo Lake glacier, among others, formed and eroded into the west-facing slopes.

13

The Glaciers of West Kill

A<small>S THE</small> G<small>RAND</small> G<small>ORGE ICE MARGIN</small> peaked, glaciers poured through gaps in the Northeastern Escarpment (see figure 18-2). Other glaciers advanced down the valley of Schoharie Creek. Ice nearly surrounded the mountains of the Central and Northeastern Escarpments, but they remained exposed, and some of the most striking landscape features formed on them. These were the *Alpine glaciers* (figure 13-1) that accumulated in mountain niches of the Northeastern and Central Escarpments. (These formations are called by various other names—*niche glaciers*, *local glaciers,* or *cirque glaciers.*)

Alpine glaciers are relatively isolated and are found away from the main continental ice sheet. They usually form in bowl-shaped cirques or niches near the summits of mountains, often on the lee side, where snow accumulates in the bowls and hardens into ice. When the ice is thick enough, it flows downhill, occupying and widening any valleys that are available. Plucking associated with the movement carves the basin of a cirque. Echo Lake is found within one of the best cirques of the Catskills. It indicates a long period of plucking.

There are not many other well-developed cirques in the Catskills, because there does not seem to have been enough time for many good ones to develop. But we do see a lot of places where proper cirques were well on their way to being carved by the Alpine glaciers. Many of them are found on the shaded north-facing slopes of the Central Escarpment, especially around Hunter Mountain. Because of its accessibility, the best one to visit is on the western slope of Hunter Mountain, at the upper reaches of the West Kill.

This Alpine glacier descended the slopes of Hunter Mountain and flowed miles down the length of the West Kill. This valley has the beautiful U-shaped profile that is typical of a valley through which glaciers have flowed (figure 13-2). Moving glaciers will carve away at a valley until this shape is achieved; the U-shape is the profile of least resistance to the flow of ice. It is one of the most typical features of an Alpine glacier, and something all glacial geologists know to look for. The West Kill

13-1. An old woodcut of an Alpine glacier.

13-2. West Kill from Hunter Mountain.

Valley earned it U-shape the hard way: First the Grand Gorge glacier advanced up the valley, then it began to melt and to retreat from the valley. Subsequently, the West Kill Alpine glacier advanced down the valley. Here, *two* glaciers helped to shape the valley (Rich, 1935).

The West Kill Valley Road leads to good, marked hiking trails which ascend from the foot of the glacier's niche to what had been the head of the ice. There are a half dozen or so places where the road rises up upon large mounds of earth which extend partially across the valley. The road generally cuts into the embankment and exposes boulder- and cobble-rich deposits (figure 13-3). Many or all of these, especially the very bouldery ones, are probably *recessional moraines* (Rich, 1935). The one lowest in the valley represents the terminus of the Alpine glacier when it descended the valley, reached a still-stand, and dropped a moraine. Then came a series of climatic fluctuations. When the climate warmed, the ice retreated, and when it cooled, the

13-3. Lake deposits (below) and moraine (above) at West Kill.

ice advanced. Each advance/retreat left a recessional moraine. This is also evident in a valley north of the town of Windham.

One of the West Kill moraines lies over an old lake deposit (figure 13-3). As the Grand Gorge glacier was retreating from the valley, it formed a dam, which impounded a small lake. The silts and clays of this deposit can be seen along Spruceton Road. Later, these deposits were disturbed by the West Kill glacier, and they are somewhat contorted.

Exploring the upper reaches and the niche of the West Kill glacier involves a rigorous hike. There are two trailheads at the end of the West Kill Road; the second one (the red trail) ascends the slopes of the niche. The trail starts out on a gentle slope, but steepens as it climbs the north side of the niche. At about 3,500 feet, there is a glacially striated ledge, which forms an overlook at the top of the niche. There is no *tarn lake* beneath, but the slopes below are quite steep. This was the plucked headwall, and with a little more time, this niche would surely have evolved into a fine cirque. It didn't, but that's not surprising—few Catskill cirques match the one at Echo Lake.

The red trail merges with the yellow trail, which leads to the top of Hunter Mountain. Hunter was a center of Alpine glaciation, and at one time Alpine glaciers were found on each of its slopes. One was found on each side of the Colonel's Chair, the main ridge of the commercial ski center. Another descended westward into West Kill. Another descended the southern slopes of the mountain and entered Stony Clove. A final one probably occupied the niche on Becker Hollow, to the northeast.

There were more Alpine glaciers on the north- and south-facing slopes of nearby Rusk Mountain. Others have been recognized on Panther Mountain and at a number of other locations throughout the central and northern Catskills, including one at East Kill.

The hiking trails of the Central Escarpment are among the most popular in the Catskills. The fire tower at the top of Hunter Mountain is an especially fine goal for a day hike, and its panoramic views are well worth it. But a knowledge of the area's glaciers offers a view of a different sort: 16,000 years ago, off to the west, you could have seen the Grand Gorge glacier advancing up West Kill Valley. Meanwhile, from the east, another great glacier was advancing eastward from Kaaterskill Clove (see figure 18-2). It passed beneath Hunter Mountain and continued on to the west. It was quite a view.

14

The Glaciers of North Lake

THERE IS A SPIRITUAL HEART to the Catskills—the area stretching from North Point to Kaaterskill Clove, which, for lack of a better term, could be called North Lake, after the state park which encompasses most of this region. North Lake may well be the most picturesque of all Catskill vicinities, with its thoroughly forested landscape dotted by fine mountains and sheltered hollows, the great clove of Kaaterskill Creek, and North and South Lakes, two of the best lakes in all the Catskills. Most of all, the area commands a sweeping eastern view of seventy miles of the Hudson River Valley. The view can be seen from anywhere along the escarpment, that sandstone ledge that makes up the crest of the Wall of Manitou.

North Lake is certainly the realm of Rip Van Winkle, for that famous Catskill story seems to have been written with this region in mind. More importantly, it is the realm of the premier resort hotel of its time, the Catskill Mountain House. Established in 1824, the hotel had reached the heights of fashion and elegance by the middle of the nineteenth century (Van Zandt, 1966). Aside from its prestige, the Mountain House attracted large numbers of people because of its picturesque landscape. The hotel was a great success.

North Lake was the domain of Charles Beach. Beach did not build the Mountain House (he was only a teenager in 1824), but he was there on the day the hotel opened. By 1839, he had a lease on the hotel, and in 1845 he bought the place. He would reign over the hotel until his death in 1902, fully 63 years. During his stewardship, hotel property expanded to more than 3,000 acres, which is virtually all of the land in the North Lake area. Beach controlled both lakes and all the land from just north of Kaaterskill Clove to North Mountain.

Today, the grounds of North Lake State Park are an ideal place for the amateur geologist to investigate the record of a glaciation. With a compass and a map, it's fairly easy to put together a pretty good picture of what the passing glaciers did here.

14-1. Eastern shore of North Lake. Striations visible.

The eastern shoreline of North Lake is the best place to start. The shores just north of the beach are of glacially scoured bedrock, and they show it (figure 14-1). Clearly they were ground down by a passing glacier—but when, and how many times? Glacial striations and crescentics provide the answers. After exploring the lake shore and collecting compass point data, several sets of striations emerge. There is a set of roughly south-oriented striations along the shores of the lake, accompanied by some crescentic gouges that also indicate a south direction. These are old and have been thoroughly worn down by later events. There are also two sets of much fresher striations. One set is oriented roughly northwest (west 20 degrees north) while the other set, seemingly the youngest, points to the southwest (west 20 to 30 degrees south). Both are curious—one would think the glaciers would have flowed south—but the directions of flow can be confirmed by the crescentic marks associated with the striations. Some of the best crescentic gouges I have ever seen were found on a bedrock surface near campsite 151 (see figure 6-3). They were fresh and only slightly weathered. (They were also buried by park workers who laid down a layer of gravel on them during the spring of 1995!) These indicated the southwestern motion.

The ledges of the Catskill Front, extending north and south of the hotel site, also show evidence of patterns of motion. Striations can be found on a number of these ledges where they are crossed by the Escarpment trail (blue). These generally trend westward, especially at higher elevations; the ice seems to have flowed out of the Hudson Valley and across the Catskill Front. Numerous erratics perch on the brink of the escarpment. These include Sunset Rock and Boulder Rock (see figures 8-2 and 8-4). These boulders speak of the movement of ice, but they do not indicate the directions of flow.

After collecting compass directions of the various sets of striations, a history of glacial motion emerges. The glaciers seem to have first moved south, parallel with the Catskill Front. This may have occurred during the original Woodfordian advance. Later, a second movement carried glaciers out of the Hudson Valley and westward across North Lake, and probably on to South Lake as well. At lower elevations this flow was influenced by the topography, and the flow was nearly northwest. At higher elevations, the flow was more nearly westward. This out-of-the-valley motion could have occurred at the time of the Wagon Wheel ice margin, but it seems more likely to be coincident with the Grand Gorge event. A similar pattern occurred on Overlook Mountain.

Curiously, here there also is a suggestion of movement from the southwest. The road that passes east of South Lake displays a good roadside outcrop, with vertically scoured and striated walls. Striations rise to the north, which suggests that the passing glacier was moving to the northeast (see figure 6-5). When did a glacier come out of the southwest? That's an interesting and puzzling problem. I don't know the answer, but that's what makes this kind of work so much fun, especially at a place like North Lake.

15

The Glaciers of Kaaterskill Clove

B<small>Y THE LATE-NINETEENTH CENTURY</small> there was a cluster
of hotels in the Catskills; by the turn of the twentieth century
there were hundreds. When the grand hotels along the Catskill
Front were in their glory, most of the greatest among them were
clustered around Kaaterskill Clove. Guests at the Catskill
Mountain House, the Hotel Kaaterskill and the Laurel House
were all only a short walk from Kaaterskill Falls and the great
clove below it. That was no accident; the clove is perhaps the
single most scenic site in all of the Catskills. Today there are no
hotels left in the area. The land is now all part of the Catskill
Forest Preserve and is owned by the state and open to the public.

The clove is a great yawning gulf, seemingly cut as a deep
gash into the Wall of Manitou. The canyon walls range from
merely steep to vertical, and they tower more than 1,000 feet
above the narrow bottom of the gorge. The gash is about half a
mile wide at its eastern mouth; the cut is about three miles long
before it tapers to a point at its western end. Any geologist will
recognize this as a typical *youthful stream*—a deep, narrow, ero-
sive river. But that is surprising and unusual in a landscape as
old as the Appalachian realm. Youthful streams are not sup-
posed to be here.

The exact age of the clove is a mystery, but there is no doubt that the clove is young; it seems to have been carved only since the Illinoian glaciation. The upper reaches of the clove may be even younger. It's been a mere 15,000 years since the Wisconsin glaciation left the clove, and the two beautiful waterfalls there seem to have formed only since then. The best one, Kaaterskill Falls, is public property and is easily accessible. The falls actually consist of two cascades separated by a platform of rock. The upper cascade is 175 feet tall; the lower one measures 85 feet. The other fine falls is Haines Falls, although it is not on public land.

Nowhere in the Catskills has glaciation impacted the scenery more than in the clove. And nowhere has the landscape influenced the development of American art more than right here. The clove trail system is virtually a museum of art. Beyond the top of Kaaterskill Falls is the beginning of the blue trail, a marked hiking trail that takes visitors along the north rim of the escarpment, then off to the southeast through the woods and on to the Layman Monument. From this site, a cut in the trees reveals a distant view of Haines Falls across the valley at the colony of Twilight Park. The trail continues and soon leads to the brink of the clove itself. From a site along this trail, Thomas Cole painted *The Clove, Catskills* in 1827.

Farther along on the trail is Inspiration Point. The point has been a favorite vantage point for hikers for more than 150 years. No wonder—on a good day the view of the clove from here is genuinely breathtaking. The view has inspired a long list of American landscape artists, including Asher Brown Durand, Sanford Robinson Gifford, Harry Fenn, and many others.

Inspiration Point is one of the best examples of *scour and pluck topography* in all the Catskills. The platform was ground to a fine polish by a passing glacier. The surface reveals numerous striations and a few grooves. Below the dance floor is a shear cliff—the plucked scar of the passing glacier. There is no doubt about which way the glacier was going, since the striations point up the clove and into the interior of the Catskills.

The glacier that penetrated here was probably associated with the Grand Gorge ice margin (see figure 18-2). Here, instead of ice overtopping the Wall of Manitou, it pressed its way up the clove. So thick and deep was the glacier that it overtopped the 2,000-foot level and continued past the clove; striations are found all the way up the valley to at least the town of Haines Falls, where the glacier fanned out and deposited a number of moraines. This was an impressive glacier, and it may have continued westward beyond Tannersville.

Farther eastward is more evidence of the glaciation. There are several more dance floors, although none of them is as impressive as the one at Inspiration Point. A spur off the trail leads to Palenville overlook, with a great view of the Hudson Valley. This is a wonderful vantage point from which to view and imagine the enormous glacier that once flowed south past this point. Actually, you don't have to rely entirely upon your imagination. The glacier scoured not only the rocks of the dance floors but also the valley floor itself. Look carefully and you will see a north-south lineation to the valley floor displayed by the fields and forests below. These lineations reflect the structure of the bedrock, which was enhanced by the scouring of passing glaciers. You are looking at the very motion of the mighty glacier that did so much to create this scene.

16

The Glaciers of East Kill

THE HOLLOW (preferably pronounced *holler*) is a staple of Appalachian folk culture. The term refers to those out-of-the-way valleys far up in the hinterlands. Here in the Catskills there are many such out-of-the-way side valleys that elude the everyday traveler. Among these is the East Kill Valley, which lies between the Blackhead Range to the north and North Mountain to the south. It's always been just a little too far away from things—too far north to be within the sphere of the Hunter Mountain ski centers, and too far south to be influenced by the Windham resorts. The valley was even too far west to have been affected by the tourist trade of the nineteenth century. It's not hard to find, nor hard to get to; it's just off the beaten path. And its upper reaches form a classic hollow.

This secluded valley is a gem. There are the mountains, of course, but there are also two fine man-made lakes at the valley's eastern terminus. There are many weekend homes along its main road, Route 23C, but otherwise it is quite picturesque. East Kill Valley has retained much of its nineteenth-century feeling, including one-room school houses, old community churches and weathered farmhouses. Many of the people who live here are descendants of the original settlers, and just by being there they seem to preserve the heritage of the valley. Most of what I know about their culture I have learned from reading Doris West Brooks' stories, which portray the valley as it was during the nineteenth century. Brooks is of the sixth generation born there, and she knows all the folklore and oral history of this tiny community. She grew up listening to much of it in her family home and she has woven all of this into her stories about East Kill.

I hadn't known much about East Kill until I read Brooks' book, *The Old Eagle Nester*. There are several features she describes in her book that aroused my curiosity. The two lakes—Colgate and Capra—obviously are man made, but I wondered if there was an older history to these basins. I was also curious about Spruce Woods swamp, the product of beaver dams—was there already a basin there before the first beaver arrived? The most interesting feature was Dutcher Pass, the deep slash cutting through the Catskill Front above the head of East Kill.

It seemed to me that there was a geological "story-behind-the-story" of East Kill that justified a hike all the way to Dutcher Pass, reached by a trail around Lake Capra to Spruce Woods, the setting for most of the stories in Brooks' book. (The Spruce Woods clearing is still there, much as it was in the last century.)

Beyond Spruce Woods is a swamp that beavers have expanded into a dammed pond. The basin that makes up the swamp is the niche that spawned an Alpine glacier. Geologists with the New York State Museum have called it the Colgate glacier, and it dates back to the time of the Grand Gorge ice margin (Dineen, 1986). From this niche the glacier flowed downhill, possibly as far as lower East Jewett, about five miles to the west.

Stretches of the valley, especially below Colgate Lake and Lake Capra, are clogged with bouldery sediment that appears to be moraine. Some or all of this material may be the product of the Colgate glacier. As the glacier melted and retreated, the recessional moraine deposits seem to have blocked the East Kill Valley and, presumably, at that time they formed earthen dams which in turn impounded the early natural lakes Capra and Colgate. These earthen dams were long ago breached by the currents of the East Kill. The old lakes were drained, but man and cement have restored what nature had destroyed.

Uphill, beyond Spruce Woods, is the old road to Dutcher Pass. Long ago, when the valley was truly isolated, this was the main road in and out of the East Kill Valley. But, like so many of the old Catskill roads, this one is now just a good hiking trail that leads to a mysterious gap in the mountain. The walls on either side of the trail steepen and close in as it ascends toward Dutcher Pass. Very large boulders of local sandstone lay in a jumble at the bottom of this ravine. It's clear what forces had created this gap in the Catskill Front: The steep slopes and large boulders spoke of an ancient whitewater stream, a spillway of glacial meltwater cascading westward down the steep slopes of Dutcher Pass, much as at Wagon Wheel Gap. An enormous, melting glacier once lay beyond the pass. Vastly larger than the Colgate glacier, this was the great glacier that once had filled the entire Hudson Valley.

For a geologist, these are exciting moments. In a flash, my imagination brought me standing before the great glacier. I could see that it was melting, and before it was a lake of ice water. A slow current flowed toward Dutcher Pass. As it approached the gap, the current speeded up. At the gap, the flow was quick but silent. Blocks of floating ice sped through the gap. Constrained at the gap, the flow widened below. Downslope, the power of the flow broke up across boulders into a thundering cascade of raging white water.

Dutcher Pass is a quiet and serene place today, but there is violence and danger to be read in this landscape.

17

The Glaciers of Windham

I<small>T IS REMARKABLE</small> just how much the recent glaciation still affects our lives today; so much of what we do during our daily routine is governed by the movements of ice a few tens of thousands of years ago. This is certainly the case with the village of Windham, a handsome old town in the northeast corner of the Catskills. During the summer the town is a serene resort area, and in the winter the village becomes a ski center. Summer or winter, you would never guess just how much the town's development has been influenced by events that occurred during the Grand Gorge ice margin, approximately 16,000 years ago.

As we have seen, the Grand Gorge glaciers formed an ice margin along the Northeastern Escarpment of the Catskill mountains. Several gaps in the escarpment provided relatively easy access, and streams of ice penetrated into the Catskills through them. Two glaciers also penetrated the escarpment in the Windham vicinity (Rich, 1935) (see figure 18-2). One glacier flowed through the gaps between Mt. Pisgah and Mt. Nebo. This stream of ice flowed down Mitchell Hollow and approached Windham from the north—let's call it the Mitchell Hollow glacier. The other glacier breached the Catskill Front through the gap at East Windham, through which Route 23 runs today. This, the East Windham glacier, flowed right over Windham, and formed a major stream of ice which evidently continued down the Batavia Kill nearly to the Schoharie Creek. Meanwhile, other glaciers were active within the Schoharie Creek Valley. Ice advanced down that valley, and some of it turned eastward and advanced up the side valley of the Batavia Kill. The Windham and Schoharie glaciers nearly collided in the vicinity of Red Falls (see figure 18-2, arrows).

After time, the climate changed and the three streams of ice melted back. The northern end of the Schoharie Creek Valley opened up, while at the same time ice retreated to the edge of the Northeastern Escarpment. This was a time when ice blocked the whole northern reach of the Schoharie Creek Valley; thus the north-flowing river was dammed. Water trapped behind this ice dam created glacial Lake Grand Gorge, and a large arm of this lake reached all the way into Windham, lapping up upon the retreating glacier (see figure 20-1). All of what is now Windham was under water. Streams flowing into Lake Grand Gorge formed deltas, and this accounts for most of what is now Windham. Much of the town is built upon the floor of that old lake; the rest is perched upon the old deltas (figure 17-1).

Some of the delta deposits are exposed north of Route 23, west of Windham. The town's main street is built upon flat lands that are a river's flood plain lying upon the floor of glacial Lake Grand Gorge. Turn right onto Church Street and cross the Batavia Kill—on the other side of the stream you will drive straight up the steep slope of the old delta front. The top of this

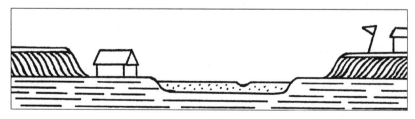

17-1. Cross section of Windham.
Diagonals: delta terraces; horizontals: lake deposits; dots: flood plain deposits.

slope is the flat top of the delta. South Road leads across the delta. Memorial Field and the Windham Country Club lie upon the delta top. When golfers tee off just west of the clubhouse, they drive their balls down the slopes of the lake floor. The hole is at the bottom of the lake. (Talk about a water hazard!)

East of the country club, the road again begins to descend another slope—this is where the glacier once abutted both the lake and its delta. After a left turn onto Route 296 north, the Pines Inn comes into view—the Pines lies upon the floor of Lake Grand Gorge. Turn left back onto Route 23 and head west. Between Bagley and Mitchell Hollow Roads there is a small hill—another old glacial lake delta. Beyond Mitchell Hollow Road, the road descends back to the floor of Lake Grand Gorge and the Windham business district built upon it. Route 23 west from the village follows the Batavia Kill, along a flat valley floor. As is usual in the Catskills, these flatlands represent flood-plains lying on old lake bottoms—this is the floor of Lake Grand Gorge. Most of the region's agriculture is on this lake bottom.

There is an interesting story behind the Mitchell Hollow glacier. This mass of ice moved south from the Mt. Pisgah gap and reached the northern edge of Windham. Then, climate fluctuations caused a series of cyclical advances and retreats of the ice. Each time the glacier advanced, it picked up and transported a mass of coarse sediment, eventually deposited as a recessional moraine. As the Mitchell Hollow glacier went through a series of advances and retreats, it produced a series of moraines that are all still there—each one is a low, curving ridge (Rich, 1935). Fortunately, the road cuts through each of them: Head north on Mitchell Hollow Road from Route 23. At 0.7, 0.9, 1.0, 1.3 and 1.5 miles you'll pass through the moraines, each a mass of cobbles, gravel and sand. The cobbles are made of red, tan and gray sandstone, while the rest of the moraine is a red sand and gravel. This is similar to what we saw in West Kill (see figure 13-3).

18

The Halls of the Schoharie

SCHOHARIE CREEK is the one large river confined entirely to the Catskill region, and it displays some of the finest scenery of our mountains. The valley is at its best in the bright warmth of early autumn. With its rural scenery, its small villages, farm stands and numerous antique shops, the Schoharie Creek Valley offers the rewards of a perfect fall afternoon drive. The best place to start such a trip is at the north end of the valley, just east of where Route 7 crosses the river. Here, where the road rises a bit above the valley, there is an unobstructed view extending about ten miles down the valley (figure 18-1). The view runs past the town of Schoharie and on to Middleburgh.

An observant geologist can see a lot of glacial geology here and can read a detailed record of the advance and retreat of glacial ice. There are two striking aspects to the landscape: the pronounced horizontal nature of the valley floor and the near-vertical slopes of some of the valley walls. Both speak of glaciation.

The striking landscape features of the area are the valley's north-south oriented slopes. They rise, almost as cliffs, above the flatness of the valley. North of Middleburgh, they are made of limestones and sandstones of the old Devonian seas. These are sturdy cliff-makers, and it is no surprise that cliffs are found here.

18-1. Schoharie Creek Valley, looking south.

It's different at Middleburgh. The bedrock here is composed of soft sandstones and shales. This is an unlikely material for a cliff, and so the question arises: Why are they here?

The story usually goes something like this: When advancing ice enters the confined space of a narrow valley, it begins to scrape the valley walls on both sides, steepening them. Given time, a steep-walled, U-shaped valley is produced—*usually* because, while a number of authors allude to this, nobody has claimed that this has produced the landscape of the Schoharie. I have talked with geologists who don't think that this has happened here. Nevertheless, I am guessing that glacial scraping and plucking had much to do the valley's landscape, especially from Middleburgh to Prattsville.

South of Middleburgh, the valley opens up again (see figure 6-1). The valley and the road turn sharply to the west, and the road hugs some very steep slopes there. The slopes rise to the finest cliff in all the Schoharie Valley—the cliff of Vromans

Nose (see figure 2-1). This is the second type of cliff found in the valley: It was plucked by a large passing glacier.

Soon the valley and its road turns south again and more tall slopes rise on either side. Below the village of Breakabeen, the character of the valley changes. Although the slopes are still steep, the valley itself narrows quite a bit, becoming most narrow between Gilboa and Prattsville. Here, more steep valley walls rise above a narrow flood plain. Beyond Prattsville, the character of the valley changes again: It broadens, and its slopes are less steep. There are few cliffs. The river also splits into a number of tributaries and their valleys, which include the East Kill and West Kill. Thus, the valley is narrow at Gilboa but wide above and below the town.

The Schoharie Creek Valley saw the passage of glaciers—but not the great ice sheet that overtopped the Catskills and proceeded to Long Island. Nor was it the substantial Wagon Wheel glaciers that swept across all of the Northeastern Escarpment. These were different glaciers; they were the glaciers of a more confined nature (Cadwell, 1986).

Ice had begun a retreat from the Wagon Wheel ice margin about 17,000 years ago. For several centuries, there was stagnant ice throughout the lower Schoharie Creek Valley. Then, perhaps about 16,500 years ago, there was another episode of active ice. Again, glaciers advanced down the Hudson River Valley, and again, they entered into the Catskills. This activity established the Grand Gorge ice margin (figure 18-2). But this time, the ice was not as thick as it had been earlier. The top of this ice sheet must have been just a little lower than the mountains of the Northeastern Escarpment. Because of this, these glaciers could not overtop the mountains, but instead were mostly funneled into the valleys, and the Schoharie Creek Valley was among the very best of those available.

As glaciers entered into the wide northern reaches of the Schoharie Creek, they were just thick enough to cover the mountains west of the valley. So most of the ice filled the valley, and a stream of advancing ice flowed within the confines of the bedrock slopes. If the ice did carve these masses of bedrock into the great hallways we see today, then this was when it happened. The hallways are most impressive where the valley had already been constricted. That may explain much of what we see in the view from Route 7 (figure 18-1). Immediately south, at Vrooman, the first set of walls is found; this may represent the squeezing of ice into a narrow valley. This process was repeated at Middleburgh, where steep rocky slopes tower above

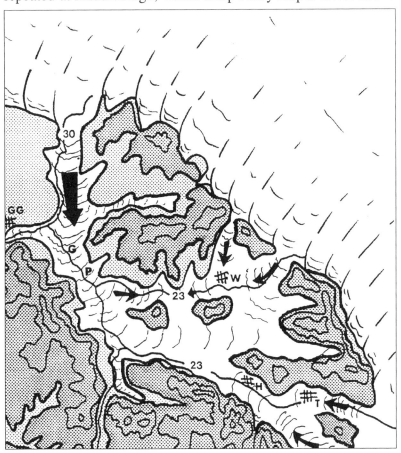

18-2. The Grand Gorge ice margin. Highways marked. Letters indicate Windham, Grand Gorge, Gilboa, Prattsville, Hunter, and Tannersville.

the town (see figure 2-1). South of Middleburgh, the glacier seems to have been steered westward by the valley walls, where it was joined by the thinner sheet of ice that had crossed the mountains west of the valley. This was the ice that crossed Vromans Nose, sculpted the dance floor and plucked the cliffs.

South of Breakabeen, the ice funneled into an even narrower valley; from Gilboa to Prattsville the Schoharie Creek Valley is at its narrowest. Here it is easy to imagine that too much ice was squeezed into too little valley—once again the ice seems to have overflowed its valley. As it crossed adjacent mountains, the ice sheet sculpted dance floors and plucked cliffs. Famous Pratt Rock mimics the plucking effect at Vromans Nose, and so does the plucked cliff on Dog Hill, one mile north of Prattsville.

Beyond Prattsville, the Schoharie Creek Valley opens up again into a broad, low-sloped valley. There are few scoured cliffs along this stretch of the valley. Here, the Grand Gorge glacier advanced easily, at least halfway up the Batavia Kill. Here, at last, the motion of the valley glacier seems to have come to a halt: It met ice advancing up Kaaterskill and Plattekill cloves (figure 18-2).

19

The Glaciers of Grand Gorge

Grand Gorge is just a quiet, western Catskill village. The name seems a misnomer; there is no obvious landscape feature here that would give the town such a name.

Grand Gorge is, of course, named for the gap found off to the south. A short distance along Route 30, the road ascends a steep incline and approaches the topographic gap—*the* grand gorge. From the road, there is no particularly good view of the gap, but the road soon passes between two slopes of rock that rise steeply several hundred feet above the valley floor.

Beyond the gap, the valley continues narrow for some distance. The valley floor is flat here, and along the road are the uppermost reaches of the East Branch of the Delaware River, sometimes called the Pepacton River (figure 19-1). Up here, the stream hardly deserves to be called a river. It consists of a number of quiet pools nearly hidden among extensive wetlands. The stream and its channel do not match; the stream is much too small for the valley. This is a classic example of an underfit stream, similar to the streams in the lower Esopus Creek Valley. Here too, there was once a much larger river, and it was this river that carved the channel of the upper Pepacton (Rich, 1935).

19-1. Grand Gorge from the south.

As in the Esopus Creek Valley, glaciers were responsible for the landscape. Ice penetrated Grand Gorge Gap at the time of the Wagon Wheel ice margin (see figure 9-1). The ice then retreated, but during the time of the Grand Gorge ice margin it still lay just north of the gap (see figure 18-2). This still-stand was followed by another melting and another retreat of the glacier. The very large river that once flowed through Grand Gorge Gap was the product of the meltwater of this retreat. The raging water carved the deeper, narrower gap (Rich, 1935).

Beyond the gap, the Pepacton must have been quite a river for a time. Evidence of it can still be found. The marshes form a broad swath of valley floor, which defines the channel of that older Pepacton River. You might say that the marshes have filled a fossil river channel. These wetlands are the key to recognizing the old river channel, and once you know how to read the landscape you can find stretches of the fossil Pepacton for some distance down the valley. The old Pepacton was much wider than today's river, and it must have been a lot deeper as well. The old Pepacton carried a very large volume of water.

Curiously, there are two notches at Grand Gorge. The second, smaller notch is just to the west of the main one. There are few good views of it, but one can be found to the south on Duggan Hill Road. This smaller notch, perched high on the slopes of the hill, was evidently carved at a time when ice blocked the main valley. Thus, this second gap is very reminiscent of Wagon Wheel Notch.

19-2. Grand Gorge from the north.

A truly panoramic view of Grand Gorge Gap can be enjoyed by traveling north through the village of Grand Gorge and continuing on Route 30 for about a half mile. Near the top of the hill is a dirt turnoff on the left; to the east are the upper reaches of the Bear Kill Valley. From this vantage point, the geological Grand Gorge is visible in the southwest (figure 19-2). The feature is impressive and out of character for the western Catskills—it is not so much a *gorge* as it is a great *gap* in the Central Escarpment of the Catskills. To the right, the smaller gap is barely visible just above the horizon. Gaps of this sort catch the eye of the geologist; they have a story to tell.

April 27, 14,105 BC

The glacier is a mess. It is not just melting; it is disintegrating. It is breaking up into a myriad of icy-blue, jagged blocks. Driving, warm rains create a thick ground fog, which is quickly blown northward across the ice. The fallen rain drains into the crevasses between the blocks, and fast currents of meltwater zigzag back and forth within the ice. From these currents, enormous and loud fountains of water are pouring out of the wide crevasses at the front of the glacier. All along the base of the ice, surging masses of meltwater are boiling up from underwater crevasses. This would be loud enough, but every few hours the air is shattered by the explosive sound of large, wet masses of slushy ice collapsing into the lake. A dense ice flow is drifting slowly toward the south. The ice is being drawn toward the distant gap by a very strong current.

The view is different from a perch above the northwest side of the Grand Gorge Gap. Below, the water currents speed up as they are sucked into the gap. As blocks of ice approach, they become crowded and interfere with the smooth flow of water. The currents break up into a noisy, whitewater froth. This is made worse by the narrowness of the gap. In effect, Grand Gorge Gap is a horizontal waterfall with its currents not falling, but squeezing between the two towering walls of rock. It is this powerful, horizontal waterfall that has carved Grand Gorge Gap.

To the south beyond Grand Gorge Gap, in the narrow upper reaches of the Pepacton, is a long, continuous roaring cataract. Down the valley it widens into a raging, foaming torrent, a landscape-carving machine. The Pepacton sweeps back and forth across its valley. Its currents have cut through all of the older glacial deposits that had clogged the valley. In a few years it will rearrange this valley, and leave a mark that will last for thousands of years.

20

Glacial Lake Grand Gorge

O<small>NE OF THE SURPRISING THINGS</small> in writing about a region's geology comes with the realization that some of the biggest geological phenomena are completely unknown to the general public. That is certainly the case with the largest glacial feature of the Catskills—glacial Lake Grand Gorge.

Glacial lakes are common in the Catskills. In fact, most Catskill lakes have some sort of glacial origin. Many have basins that were, in one way or another, created by glacial scouring or deposition, and some were dammed by the ice itself. The best remaining ones are Lake Otsego at Cooperstown, and nearby Canadarago Lake. There are also many small glacial lakes, such as Echo Lake. But historically there were many more, and Lake Grand Gorge was the biggest of them all (figure 20-1).

The story of Lake Grand Gorge goes back to the end of the Grand Gorge ice margin. The ice had flooded the valley of the Schoharie Creek, but as it began to melt, voluminous meltwater was produced, but with few opportunities for drainage. Schoharie Creek could have carried the water off to the north, but the creek was blocked by a thick sheet of ice. So drainage had to be away from the glacier, which meant to the south.

What resulted was a repeat of the story of the notches. For a while, rising levels of ice water must have pooled around the edges of the melting valley glacier, and soon the water began to pour through the Grand Gorge Gap. The gap had previously been active at the end of the Wagon Wheel ice margin, when a tongue of ice passed through it. Now, during this younger (more recent) glacial phase, it would be reused—the waters of the Pepacton would rise into a whitewater torrent, draining into the Delaware River basin, the valley loud with the river's roar.

The lake started out small, but expanded with time. In spite of all the water pouring through the gap, there was quite a large lake

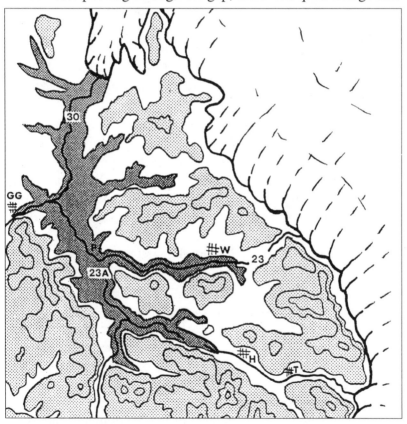

20-1. Map of North Blenheim ice margin and glacial Lake Grand Gorge. Highways marked. Letters indicate Grand Gorge, Windham, Hunter, and Tannersville.

20-2. Foreset beds of delta terrace.

forming north between the gap and the melting glacier. At its greatest, it filled much of the Schoharie Creek Valley, extending from around North Blenheim in the north all the way to Hunter in the south. Branches of the lake extended into several of the tributary valleys of the Schoharie. The Batavia Kill was completely flooded, as was the West Kill, Manorkill and part of East Kill.

Generally, ice melted around the edges of a lake first, and the large bulk of the ice was left throughout its central expanse. In the shaded backwaters of Lake Grand Gorge these large masses of ice probably survived for quite a long time, choking several branches of the lake. This was year-round ice, which means Lake Grand Gorge was a very different sort of lake from what we are used to.

Numerous streams descended the slopes of the lake shore. The waters were dirty with sediment washing off the bare, thawing slopes. Where streams entered into the lake, they deposited their sediments as deltas. A lake delta deposit is composed mostly of sand and has a characteristic morphology: The delta has a sloping front, and sand, deposited on that slope, accumulates as inclined sheets or strata. Where sand and gravel pits cut into deltas, these beds, called *foresets*, are easy to spot (figure 20-2). Above the foresets are a few feet of flat-lying strata called *topsets*, which are deposited in very shallow water—thus the delta tops mark the old lake levels. Thus, if you can find the old deltas, it is easy to map the old lake.

We know a lot about the old shoreline of Lake Grand Gorge, but I know of no published research map of the lake. The map here is drawn with the lake level being at about 1,600 feet. The map is a compromise, but it is not likely to be off by too much. The base of Grand Gorge Gap started at an elevation of 1,640 feet and was eroded to 1,560 feet (Rich, 1935). The lake level dropped accordingly. This is reflected in the fact that the delta tops range between those two levels.

As time passed, the glacier continued to melt and its front continued to retreat northward through the Schoharie Valley. For a time it stalled at West Conesville, and left a moraine there. Then it retreated relatively rapidly north to the vicinity above North Blenheim, where it stagnated again and left another moraine (Cadwell, 1986). Each retreat left space for an even larger Lake Grand Gorge. Furthermore, the northward retreat opened up other valleys; the Batavia Kill and Manor Kill thawed out and filled up with water, each becoming substantial arms of the growing lake. Finally, the Mine Kill, Platter Kill and Keyser Kill were added to the list. It was a big lake, but it didn't last long.

21

The View from Vromans Nose

FOR THE MOST PART, the towering slopes of the hallways of Schoharie Creek are too steep for many people to climb. There is one place, however, where one of these heights is accessible— it's a small hill with the curious name of Vromans (or, if you like, Vroomans) Nose. Vromans Nose, although small, is the gem of the Schoharie Creek Valley; it is one of the dominating landscape features that appears as you drive Route 30 north from Blenheim (see figure 2-1). The south-facing slope is a plucked cliff, and the plateau capping the hill was carved by the scouring of passing glaciers (see figure 6-6). Glacial sculpturing may have occurred during all of the glacial advances that crossed the Catskills, but the nose, as we know it today, is probably the product of the movement of ice toward the Grand Gorge ice margin.

Vromans Nose is a forever-wild refuge, open to the public and administered by a private foundation. That might not have been, however. By the early 1980s, two houses had already been developed close to the summit, and there was talk of a motel at the very peak. Local people, including members of the Vroman family, organized and raised the funds to buy the land, and to this day they maintain the park. On paper, it is the Vromans Nose Corporation that runs things, but in reality, it is people like Wally Van Houten

21-1. The view from Vromans Nose.

who do the work. I met Wally at his home across the highway from the nose and he showed me the summit. A retired earth science teacher, Wally has a real appreciation for the old mountain, and he is proud of what his group has accomplished here.

The top of Vromans Nose can be reached by any of three trails. A red trail runs right up the face of the steep, south slope—a difficult climb for most people. The easy trail is the green one; it ascends the gentle western slopes of the mountain. An intermediate trail, the blue one, ascends the eastern slopes. (I like to go up the green and down the blue.)

The climb is worth the effort. At the top is the dance floor, with its spectacular view of the entire lower Schoharie Creek Valley (figure 21-1). A hike on a warm, sunny afternoon in early autumn, just as the leaves reach their peak of color, will not soon be forgotten.

The geological aesthetics of the nose are available all year. Below, the floor of the Schoharie Creek is broad and flat. Read this landscape and you can find the record of the floor of glacial Lake Grand Gorge (see figure 6-1). The story picks up from the last chapter. As the glacier that had been damming Schoharie

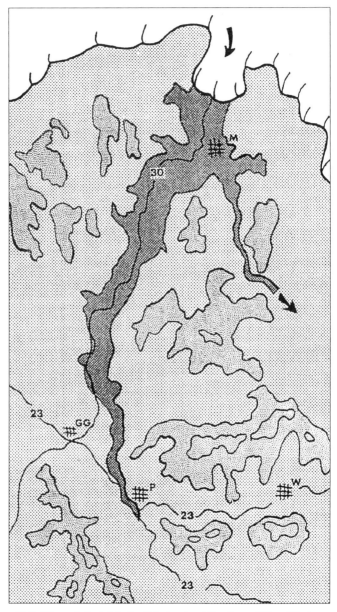

21-2. Map of glacial Lake Schoharie at the time of Franklinton drain; Middleburgh readvance. Highways marked. Letters indicate Grand Gorge, Prattsville, Windham, and Middleburgh.

Creek continued its retreat north, glacial Lake Grand Gorge expanded in the same direction. It is also likely that much of the ice in the various tributary valleys was also melting. All of this melting provided fresh meltwater which continued to drain through the gap at Grand Gorge. But, something important happened as the glacier that filled this valley retreated to the vicinity of Middleburgh: A new drainage pattern became available. Meltwater drained into Little Schoharie Creek (figure 21-2), and from there into the upper reaches of Catskill Creek. While water had been draining through Grand Gorge at about 1,600 feet, it could now drain into Catskill Creek at about 1,170 feet. Naturally, it did so (Cadwell, 1986).

In a very short time, the lake level dropped about 430 feet, and drainage through Grand Gorge Gap stopped altogether. Practically overnight, the Pepacton River went from a raging whitewater stream to the quiet, sluggish stream we see today. Meanwhile, the lower Schoharie Creek saw the same 430-foot drop in the lake level. When all of this was completed, glacial Lake Grand Gorge had shrunk considerably. In fact, it is not appropriate to use the same name for the smaller lake—the name for this one is glacial Lake Schoharie (figure 21-2).

The history gets complex here. The climate fluctuated back and forth between warm and cold. The Schoharie Creek glacier retreated far north, readvanced (called the *Middleburgh Readvance*), then retreated once more. Through all this, Glacial Lake Schoharie expanded and contracted. Finally, the glacier retreated to the Mohawk River Valley and the waters of the Schoharie drained off into the Mohawk Valley.

The interesting thing about Vromans Nose during this time is that the summit of the nose stood about 1,220 feet, while Lake Schoharie lay at about 1,170 feet. Thus, the dance floor of today's mountain and its steep cliff face must have formed a most beautiful cliffed shoreline of glacial Lake Schoharie. And for a while behind that lake shore, Vromans Nose must have been Vromans Island!

Vromans Island, June 7, 13,505 BC, just before dawn

The first glimmerings of dawn are showing above the eastern horizon, where the sky grades from a dark blue above to a cream-colored horizon. Just off to the northeast looms the enormous wall of a glacier's front. The upper facets of ice are high enough to be catching a lot of the early morning light, and they are bright with snowy whiteness. In between those facets, the ice is still dark blue; below, the ice is dark and featureless.

As the eastern sky lightens, the landscape begins to appear. It is actually a large, deep, frozen lake, mostly covered with a thick blanket of snow. To the west, the snow has blown up onto the shore, and then up onto the low slopes of the hill. That's the case as far as you can see along the western shore of the lake. To the east, however, the view is different—here the whiteness abruptly ends, and a large channel of water can be seen. This channel is black in the dim morning light, but the blackness is interrupted by the clear images of white cakes of floating ice. The ice of Lake Schoharie has been melting and breaking up; a small armada of its pieces is drifting to the northeast.

There are no animals, birds or insects anywhere in this vicinity. The air is absolutely still this morning, and there should be no noise whatsoever, but that is not the case. There is an intermittent creaking, groaning and sharp cracking from the glacier. Also there is a steady sound, a muffled roar, to the east. The dark current of water, with its drifting ice flow, is pointing the way to the source of this roar—a flow of water draining down the valley leading to Franklinton. Beyond Franklinton are the upper reaches of Catskill Creek, and all of the water of Schoharie is pouring down that stream.

*The glacier is in full advance. Over the past several winters the weather has been mild and humid. Enormous amounts of snow have fallen upon the Laurentide Ice Sheet. All this new snow has pressed down upon it and helped drive it southward, and a lot of ice has wedged into the Schoharie Creek Valley. Beneath the glacier, the warm conditions have produced a lot of meltwater. This has accumulated within the soft muds at the base, and the hydrostatic pressure of this water has given the ice just a little lift off of the valley floor. The glacier, in effect, has been hydroplaning down the valley at a remarkable velocity, up to 90 meters per day. This is called a **surging glacier**.*

This is also a time of melting ice, and the results are predictable. The tall wall of ice that makes up the front of the Schoharie Valley glacier towers above the thin cover of ice on the lake. Its steepness and great weight make it unstable, and enormous masses of wet ice give way and crash down into the lake. A huge wave of water erupts from this impact, and the great wave begins to radiate out across the lake. This wave is big, but it faces a problem—the lake is frozen over and the wave is trapped beneath the ice. Soon, closely spaced, concentrically curved fractures appear within the ice, one after another, as the wave front expands across the lake. As each fracture opens up, a geyser-like hissing wall of water erupts and splashes back down upon the ice. This continues until the wave reaches the other side of the lake and then, banking off of the lake shore, the wave front begins to advance to the south. As it does more fractures appear.

Now the lake is a real mess: An enormous hodgepodge of floe ice is drifting back and forth, buffeted by the churned up water and waves. In an hour or so, the lake will settle down, but the currents will continue to slowly carry all of the fresh floe ice toward the narrow Franklinton outlet. There, an ice jam already will be forming, and water will begin to back up behind this dam. The flow down the outlet will slow to a trickle, and once again it will be quiet.

22

Retreat in the West

While the glaciers were retreating through the eastern and central Catskills, leaving evidence of their pauses at the major ice margins, they were doing much the same in the western Catskills. But, because the landscape of the western Catskills is different, so too was the nature of its glaciers' retreat (Fleisher, 1991).

In a mountainous region, the front of a retreating continental glacier does not melt evenly. There is a point at which the peaks are sunlit and relatively warm, while the valleys are shaded and cold. Thus ice melts off the mountains and hills while the valleys continue to support the glaciers.

There was another complexity that was very important to this type of ice sheet: Even though there was melting all along the front of the ice sheet, there still may have been a great deal of snow and ice piling up to the north, where ice accumulated and moved south toward the front. Streams of ice, often called *ice tongues*, were replenished from the north and protruded southward down the valleys well beyond the main ice sheet. These valley glaciers must have been fabulous sights to see—some of them are thought to have been more than ten miles long, great rivers of ice flowing down the major valleys of the western

Catskills. Thus, even though the Laurentide Ice Sheet was melting, valley fingers of its ice were still actively advancing. This is called an *active ice* front.

Alternatively, there were times of little or no snow accumulation in the north, and the glacier didn't move much. Such a glacier is said to be composed of *stagnant ice*. This inactive ice could not advance down a valley; instead, it passively thinned while melting along its warm southern front, and its margin quickly retreated. It appears that Catskill valley glaciers typically went through numerous cycles of alternating active and stagnant ice.

All of this shows in the landscape. There is a big difference between valley landscapes produced by active and stagnant glaciers. An active glacier displays a "conveyor belt" effect, and continues to transport rock debris toward the melting front. If there is a balance between the rate at which ice advances and the rate at which it melts, this will produce an active but stationary ice margin; sand or boulders will be transported to the front and left there in a growing heap as the ice melts away (figure 22-1). These hummocky piles are composed of very coarse-grained,

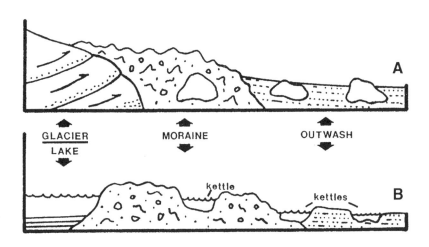

22-1. Origin of a terminal or recessional moraine, outwash plain and kettle lake.
A: longitudinal view; B: after ice retreats.

mixed sediment, and they come in a wide variety of morphologies. As these represent only a short pause in the retreat of the ice, the most useful term for them is recessional moraine.

Glaciers shed a lot of water, and this meltwater flows through the moraine and sweeps off the finer sediments, most of which are sands and silts. These sediments accumulate a short distance down the valley as a stratified deposit called an *outwash plain* (figures 22-1 and 22-2). Such a plain generally slopes away from the glacier front at a low angle. It's often pitted with small ponds called *kettle lakes* that were left as blocks of ice melted (see figure 25-3).

A large moraine will usually produce a large outwash deposit, and the two can eventually clog an entire valley. It is common in the western Catskills to encounter stretches of valleys clogged with these moraine/outwash complexes. Some modern streams have been forced to flow through narrow canyons that they have carved through such debris (figure 22-3).

22-2. Stratified outwash deposit.

But stagnant ice doesn't exhibit any of these mechanics. It is entirely inactive; there is no conveyor-belt effect that brings sediment to its front. No heaps of sediment accumulate there, and no recessional moraines or outwash plains are formed.

Often, an episode of active ice creates a moraine, followed by stagnant ice retreat. As the ice front melts, the recessional moraine is likely to block the valley entirely and act as an earthen dam. A meltwater glacial lake will form behind that dam as the ice front recedes. Meanwhile, lake sediments will accumulate. This sediment, mostly silt and clay, is transported down the valley, carried by a strong, subglacial flow of meltwater. The material, sort of a liquefied mud, emerges at the base of the glacier and fills in the valley lowlands. The magnitude of this process is truly remarkable. In the Susquehanna Valley of the Oneonta region there is rarely less than 150 feet of lake bottom sediment spread across the valley floor (Fleisher, 1991). These sediments settle into roughly horizontal sheets on the floor of the lake, and soon the lake bottom becomes quite flat (most lake bottoms are). The lake will last until its earthen dam is cut through by stream erosion, but that is likely to take a while.

Long after the glaciers are melted and the lakes have drained, these flat landscapes become ideal places for river flood plains to develop. Flat flood plains develop upon flat lake bottoms and this results in the often marshy valley floors so common in the Catskills. Typically, rivers meander freely across these surfaces. Unobtrusive as valley flats are, they constitute one of the most important glacial landscape features of the Catskills (figure 22-4).

The glacial terraces, which are often found on both sides of the valley flat, are also very important glacial features in the western Catskills. They are often nearly flat-topped and composed of internally sloping strata of gravel. There are several ways they can form. Often there are meltwater streams flowing down either side of the glacier. Sediment washed down to the glacier is caught up in these streams and swept down the valley and into the glacial lake. These sediments accumulate along the

22-3. Clogged valley at Cooperstown.

22-4. Dead ice landscape south of Stamford.

22-5. Terraces.

retreating ice as a continuous delta which stretches down the valley. After the lake waters drain, these features are left behind as what are commonly called *delta terraces*. Sediment washing off the hill slopes may also contribute to these delta terraces. Even dirty meltwater flowing through subglacial tunnels may carry sediment to such terraces. In fact, the latter may be the most significant source of these features. Delta terraces are important; today we see them as very prominent features stretching along the sides of many western Catskill valleys (figure 22-5).

All of this activity describes what happened in the valley of the Susquehanna. The hills on either side of the river emerged from the once-thick ice, while a very substantial stream of ice still filled the valley. Sometimes that valley ice was active, moving as a stream of ice down the valley and bringing enormous heaps of debris to its melting terminus. Stretches of valleys clogged with sediment are left from such times. At other times, the valley ice was stagnant and passively melted away, leaving terraces and valley fill behind. Broad, flat valley floors remain from such episodes.

March 21, 13,505 BC, early morning

*The mind's eye is east of Oneonta, in the western Catskills, drifting high above the valley of the Susquehanna River, which, on this day of the equinox, is brightly sunlit. To the north and east of Oneonta is the Laurentide Ice Sheet. To the south and west is a landscape that is barren, but at least not covered in ice. Farther south there are shrubs, then trees, and then forests, but they have not yet caught up to the retreating glacier. Although the hills here have recently escaped the grip of the retreating Laurentide ice, the valleys have not. Immediately below, a very long, narrow valley glacier extends westward many miles down the Susquehanna River Valley. The ice nearly fills the valley. Downstream and off to the west, several creeks descend the hill slopes; some flow onto the ice and continue westward along each side of the glacier. They don't get very far before they melt their way into the ice and disappear as subglacial streams. This is a **temperate glacier**—its ice is nearly at the melting point, and it cannot support a surface stream for long.*

At its terminus, the glacier is melting. The ice thins and gradually slopes down to the shore of a long, narrow lake which extends farther down the valley. A retreating glacier of this sort is much like one of those great paving machines that the highway department uses. As such a machine moves up the road, it leaves behind a flat pavement of asphalt. Similarly, the retreating glacier leaves a "pavement" of sediment.

And there is deposition going on all along the glacier's terminus, with much sediment piling up within the lake. On each shore of the lake there is a low, gravelly mud flat. These are the deltas of those subglacial streams flowing from above. They emerge from the ice here, and then they split up into a complex, criss-crossing network of shallow channels flowing across the deltas and emptying into the lake.

All along the front of the ice the lake waters are gray; powerful currents of dirty water are welling up into the lake, rising from below the ice. On this day the rising currents are strong, and the dirty water churns and boils. Many fine silts and clays are being added to the lake bottom.

It is a fabulous view; it is a view of a continental ice sheet in full retreat.

23

Retreat Along the Susquehanna

THE DREAM OF MANY an ardent baseball fan is a visit to Cooperstown. Anyone who approaches this sainted town from the south or west will likely travel along the Susquehanna Valley. The route is a good one for the ardent glacier fan as well—there are many fine glacial features to be observed on the way. Whether you're searching for baseball or glacial history, it is a most scenic trip, especially during the summer and early autumn.

The Susquehanna River Valley was one of the major access routes for glaciers to enter the Catskills. We have already seen others at Schoharie Creek and Esopus Creek. The upper Susquehanna cannot match these for size, but its narrow, shaded valleys were ideal for the development of valley glaciers. This landscape makes a very good "read."

Let's pick up the story in the village of Wells Bridge. The town, a small, modest western Catskill village, is built upon a well-preserved recessional moraine/outwash plain complex. Approaching Wells Bridge from the east, the valley narrows. The glacier had been retreating up the Susquehanna when, about 16,000 years ago, its retreat halted for a substantial still-stand; the recessional moraine that was produced is called the *Wells Bridge moraine* (Fleisher, 1977). The valley here is choked with the sediment of the moraine, and this stretch of the valley is a typical active ice landscape.

The valley east toward Otego reads of the retreat of stagnant ice—it is broad and flat, the perfect image of a glacial lake bottom and modern flood plain. The Wells Bridge moraine blocked the valley thoroughly and made an effective earthen dam. Waters were impounded behind it in what has been called glacial Lake Otego. For about ten miles east, the lake floor/flood plain is the dominant landscape feature. On either side of the valley are fine delta terraces. As the ice melted, dirty water emerged from the northern and southern sides of the glacier and deposited these delta-form structures into the lake. (These features are more continuous and better developed on the north side of the valley, and when Route 7 was built, the engineers took advantage of this—the road lies well above any flood hazard.) All of the delta terraces reach an elevation of about 1,140 feet, which is probably the old lake level. The valley bottoms out at 1,050 feet, so Lake Otego must have been at least 100 feet deep. (Actually, it was considerably deeper than that—there are hundreds of feet of lake sediment beneath the surface here.)

There are two good roads to travel east toward Oneonta. One, Route 7, will take you along the delta terraces, but the other, Interstate 88, will give you a better feel for the broad, flat, old lake bottom, especially west of Oneonta.

There was at least one very large delta in Lake Otego upon which Oneonta, the biggest town of the area, was built. Oneonta Creek and Silver Creek both flowed into the lake here, and their combined delta is quite sizable. The topset beds of the delta were deposited approximately even with the old lake waters, creating a flat landscape at about the 1,140-foot level. The center of Oneonta was built on this delta's topset, and it is elevated well above the lake floor and its flood hazards. The term *hanging delta* is often used for a delta left high and dry like this one.

For about a mile, from the east end of Oneonta almost to Emmons, there is another recessional moraine. Route 7 is built upon this, and several kettle lakes can be seen from the road. Near Emmons, the road descends off the moraine and onto a fine delta terrace. The terrace extends eastward to Cooperstown Junction, where it has a match on the other side of the valley. There is a thriving sand and gravel industry here as well. These terraces are best seen from I-88, north of the road. Here the terraces top out at 1,180 feet; thus, there seems to have been another glacial lake here, smaller and a bit higher than Lake Otego. There is a relatively narrow lake floor/flood plain here below the terraces.

The valley of the Susquehanna soon turns north, and Route 28 follows the river north toward Cooperstown. Just beyond the turn is the dam that impounds Goodyear Lake. This site is where another moraine/outwash plain complex begins; it is a stretch of the valley characterized by active ice features. Goodyear Lake is right in the midst of an outwash plain deposit. The lake itself occupies the former locations of a number of kettle lakes that were buried in outwash deposits. Some of the outwash can be seen in a gravel pit along the road—a very coarse and cobble-rich deposit. The moraine itself is located a bit to the north at Portlandville. (Cross the bridge at Portlandville and head north. First you will cross a broad flat plateau—the outwash plain. Then the landscape becomes more hummocky—that's the moraine. We'll see this again just south of Cooperstown.)

There is a broad, flat, low, marshy area north of Goodyear Lake that does not match the landscape upstream or downstream. This vicinity was where a huge block of ice once laid, partly buried by glacial deposits. The ice was a great chunk of the valley glacier that detached during its melting. After the ice melted, a hole was left, which soon was filled in by flood plain deposits. Such features are called *dead ice sinks*. It's really a very big kettle (Fleisher, 1986).

Beyond Portlandville the valley opens up again into another old lake bottom. Thus we reach a stretch of the valley that is a stagnant ice landscape. This was glacial Lake Milford. Route 28 follows the old lake's delta terraces. The low-lying valley center is typical lake floor/flood plain landscape; it is marshy and the river meanders sluggishly here. Milford (north of Milford Center) is built upon yet another broad elevated delta. Here the elevation of the delta's topset beds is about 1,220 feet, and from this we can deduce the level of the lake waters. Glacial Lake Milford was higher than the lakes down the valley.

More trees and gravel pits, as well as another short stretch of clogged valley, can found to the north of Milford. Lake Milford extended beyond that, all the way to Hyde Park.

24

The Glaciers of Council Rock

TIMES CHANGE. All places, all landscapes, have very long histories and are the sites of continuous change. Geologists are acutely aware of this, and are always on the lookout for places to read the many signs and vestiges of the past. Cooperstown lies in one of those places.

The Cooperstown of the past bears little resemblance to the present town. Today, Cooperstown, the site of the National Baseball Hall of Fame, is a tourist Mecca for baseball fans, especially in the summer. You can find places named The Home Plate, The Seventh Inning Stretch, The Dugout, The Short Stop, and The National Pastime. What else would you expect in a town that has a baseball field right in the heart of its downtown district?

While baseball dominates the town today, there are still bits and pieces of the town's more distant history. The upper stories of the Main Street buildings still show the architectural touches of the Victorian-age Main Street. Some of them are still quite beautiful, with carved Catskill bluestone and Triassic red sandstone facades. Then there is the eighteenth-century leatherstocking country legacy—the times made famous by the fiction of James Fenimore Cooper and by the real history of important campaigns of the Revolutionary War. Historic markers at the bridge across the Susquehanna River record General James Clinton's 1779 campaign against the English and their Native American allies.

Clinton's fleet of small riverboats had been carried overland from the Mohawk Valley. Clinton was on his way to join General Sullivan's forces farther down the Susquehanna, but Clinton's troops were stalled at the shallow mouth of the river. They built a dam and raised the level of the lake. Then, with all of the boats in the river, they broke the dam and rode the flood down to deeper stretches of the Susquehanna.

General Clinton's dam break was quite a feat, and is a well-recorded part of Cooperstown's history. Few people know, however, that Clinton's flood was only a pale imitation of a much greater dam break in the lake's geological history.

That ancient flood was a part of the geological legacy of Cooperstown, one which can be contemplated in the small Council Rock Park near the mouth of the Susquehanna River. An old bluestone stairway leads down to a platform looking out onto the lake shore. The site has a fine prospect of Otsego Lake and Council Rock itself; it's a good place to sit and ponder questions about the past.

The answers to these questions take us back about 14,000 years, when the view from the Council Rock site was quite different from the one we see today (Fleisher, 1977). The landscape was entirely different; Cooperstown was recovering from the passing of the Laurentide Ice Sheet. The vicinity had been completely inundated with ice at the peak of the glaciation, but the glacier melted back well to the north. Even the valley glaciers were gone. It was still too cold, however, for trees to become re-established. Instead, the region was a grassy, weedy landscape called a *tundra*—a barren landscape covered with a thin foliage of lichens, mosses and some flowering plants. Tundras are usually found immediately south of glaciated landscape, which was the case here. This regrowth was the best that nature could do to "reforest" the land in the brief time that had been available. (It is possible that temperate climates with their forests closely followed the retreating glaciers. If so, then there was no tundra at this time. The evidence is not all in yet.)

There were other imprints in the landscape left by the Laurentide Ice Sheet. Before the glaciers advanced, the landscape had been more rugged. Peaks had been higher and sharper, and the valleys had been deeper and narrower. After the glacier, the landscape, especially the hilltops, was smoothed out quite a bit. The basin of today's Otsego Lake is hundreds of feet deep, and it was only after the latest glaciation that much of it came to be filled in with sediment. So it is likely that there was some sort of an older Otsego Lake that predates the present one.

Recovery from the glaciation would be stifled because, once again, the climate was getting colder. This time there were no forests to be killed; the tundra foliage was well adapted to the cold and it did relatively well. Visible change, however, would come to other elements in the environment. At the northern end of the lake is a hill called the Sleeping Lion. The "lion" lies there with its head resting on its outstretched right foreleg. There must have been a day when, to the lion's west, a fringe of white appeared on the horizon. The white did not seem to move, but in a matter of time it grew clearer on the horizon and focused into the image of a glacier. Eventually the glacier curled around the west side of the lion and advanced southward. Then another curl of white moved around the east side of the lion. The two glaciers joined forces, south of the lion, and moved rapidly (by glacier standards) toward Cooperstown.

The profile of the ice expanded and grew taller. This was not just another valley glacier—ice was appearing over the adjacent hills as well—this was a major readvance of the ice sheet, maybe not as big as the Woodfordian event, but very big. It would cover all of the landscape from the bottom of the valleys to above the top of the hills.

The glacier overran Cooperstown. Then, about two miles to the south, it hesitated. A return of a warmer climate brought enormous melting, and the glacier began to break up. Later, after a brief retreat, colder conditions returned. The front of the glacier became active again and soon stabilized at what is today the south shore of Lake Otsego. There was a delicate balance between the cold of the north and the warmth of the south. While the front of the glacier was stable, the ice behind it was dynamic, and it remained noisy and mobile. The ice kept shoving forward, but the effort to advance was futile because masses of dirty, blocky ice tumbled off the front of the melting glacier just as fast as it moved forward. Torrents of water from the melting ice flowed down the Susquehanna, off to the south. But most of the sand and gravel and all of the boulders were deposited near the front of the ice. Looking something like a wet, icy moonscape, large, isolated blocks of ice protruded above the gravelly sands. It was a classic still-stand that produced a fine moraine.

Another warming caused a general retreat of the glacier. The newly deposited heaps of sediment formed an earthen dam that clogged a mile or so of the valley. All of today's Cooperstown is built upon this mound of earth.

As the glacier retreated, water was impounded behind this moraine and a lake was formed. This was a bigger and deeper version of modern Otsego Lake, called Lake Cooperstown. At several locations around the lake are hanging deltas. The two best ones are at Three Mile and Five Mile Points. Viewed from the south when there is no foliage, Five Mile Point presents a fine profile of an old delta. It displays a flat topset, and its foreset slopes steeply into the modern lake. The elevations of these topsets are about 50 feet above the present level of the lake, and we can deduce that glacial Lake Cooperstown was that much deeper.

The earthen dam would hold for a while until the Susquehanna carved a canyon through it, draining the top fifty feet of water, leaving the lake at the level it is today.

General Clinton's ingenious feat of 1779 pales against this natural phenomenon.

25
The Upper Susquehanna
Lake Chain

THE UPPER SUSQUEHANNA is a remarkably typical river.
The trunk stream branches into a series of tributaries which, in
turn, branch themselves into smaller streams and creeks. This is
called a *dendritic drainage* system, and it is nature's most commonly observed river pattern.

We have seen that while glaciers were retreating from the
region they paused from time to time, and during these still-
stands they deposited recessional moraines which dammed the
various valleys. This is a very common way for glacial lakes to
be formed, and there is no place in the Catskills where there
were more of these lakes than in the upper Susquehanna basin.

The major branches of the upper Susquehanna include
Charlotte Creek, Schenevus Creek, Cherry Valley and Fly Creek.
In all of these systems, recessional moraines blocked the valleys
and created lakes (figure 25-1) (Fleisher, 1977), though the only
two lakes remaining are Otsego and Canadarago. All the other
lakes drained when streams eroded canyons through the moraines.
Thus, the old lake floors and other glacial lake features are now
exposed. It is a peculiar and remarkable thing to be able to travel
along side or across an old lake bottom. These are important
Catskill landscapes and they soon become very easy to read.

Along County Route 166, northeast of Milford, is the realm of glacial Lake Middlefield, which once filled Cherry Valley all the way to Roseboom. There may have actually been two lakes here; a recessional moraine crosses the valley at the village of Middlefield, and there seems to have been one lake upstream and another downstream.

Route 166 from Milford to Cherry Valley displays all of the features we expect to see remaining from an old glacial lake: the flat lake floor/flood plain and the delta terraces; here and there some small hanging deltas.

But our main attractions are along Route 28. To the north of Milford, Route 28 rises to avoid a short stretch of the valley clogged with active ice debris. Lake Milford extended beyond that, all the way to Hyde Park. At the village of Hartwick there is an especially wide delta terrace. There has been a lot of recent development on this raised flat surface.

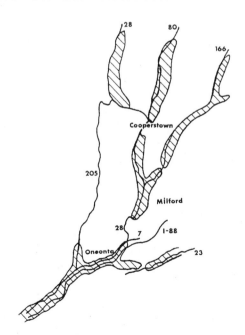

25-1. Upper Susquehanna lake chain. Major highways marked.

A few miles north on Route 28 is another moraine/outwash complex. This is an important one and it is the best displayed of them all. An excellent view is gained by turning west (left) onto County Route 26 and stopping at the top of the hill. All around is a particularly beautiful, rolling landscape. (The best time to view it is in the early morning or late afternoon, when the sun shines in at a low angle and the shadows highlight the landscape.) In early light, the hills and dales are seen as gorgeous, sinuous curves of green (figure 25-2), made more obvious by the domesticated nature of the farm fields. Most of the fields here are planted in closely-cropped grass, and this helps reveal the form of the land.

This is the Cassville-Cooperstown moraine, one of the finest moraine landscapes in the region. These great hummocks of earth, called *kames*, were brought here by a major readvance of the Laurentide Ice Sheet. This moraine is most clearly displayed here, below Cooperstown. Elsewhere it's not so obvious, but it can be traced miles to the west, to the town of Cassville. To the east, it has been correlated with the Middleburgh readvance of the Schoharie Valley.

Once, a glacier loomed over this landscape, its ice abutting against these piles of earth. At that time, some of the ice laid beneath the gravel, insulated from the heat of the sun by the blanket of sediment, long enough for even more sediment to pile up upon it. After this buried ice melted, the blankets of sediment collapsed upon the ground beneath and took on the sinuous curves displayed today. It is a classical example of *kame and kettle landscape*. It's the perfect moraine, and it is a landscape almost to be savored.

This moraine complex extends from Route 26 all the way to Cooperstown. There are several locations south of Cooperstown where rivers have eroded canyons through the moraines. The best one is the park at Council Rock, and immediately downstream, at the bridge (see figure 22-3). There are several other locations, just south of town where roads cross the river, where the narrow, canyon-like landscape has been created by a river cutting through a moraine complex.

25-2. Rolling moraine landscape south of Cooperstown.
Outwash plain in distance

25-3. Kettle lake, south of Cooperstown.

Immediately to the southwest of the Route 26 vantage point is a flat-bottomed, marshy depression (figure 25-3). This had been a *kettle lake*, but marsh deposits have filled it in. There is another kettle to the south, and still another very fine one down the road.

Kettle lakes are left behind by retreating valley glaciers. Most of them are found in moraine/outwash complexes. When they first appeared, kettle lake basins had little or no sediment in them. But they eventually accumulated layers of clay, and as the kettle pond ecology changed, thick deposits of partially decomposed plant material, called *peat*, formed. Throughout these clay-peat sequences, grains of pollen are found. Plant species can be identified from their pollen, and by studying the successive layers, a forest history is revealed. This is tedious and painstaking work, but it is very rewarding research, because these vegetative sequences provide a detailed picture of how the forests returned to New York State after the ice retreated.

The first plant ecologies to follow the ice may have been those of the tundra. However, little of this ecology is ever preserved. Kettles were likely to have been filled with ice during this time and no evidence of a tundra can be found in them. What is found is the pollen from the first forest ecologies that followed the tundra. In the austere language of science, they are referred to as being "time A forests," dominated by spruce, pines and birch. Interestingly, there is considerable charcoal in time A sediments and they seem to record a relatively warm, dry post-glacial climate. This climate was conducive to occasional fires.

The forests of the Catskills eventually re-established themselves, with the original spruce and pine forests gradually giving way to a more diverse species—oaks, maples, beech, hickory, chestnuts and elms. Later, hemlocks became dominant, and were found with pine, oak, elm and chestnut. The forests of the Catskills began to look as they would when European settlers appeared thousands of years later. All through this time, the kettle lakes patiently recorded the history.

26

Drumlins Along the Mohawk

Geomorphology is the science of landscape and is a field based upon studies conducted all over the world. That's why its jargon is studded with an abundance of exotic terminology—*yardangs* and *fensters*, *hoodoos* and *yazoos*. I think my favorite may be *drumlin*. The word is Gaelic and, in that language, it means hill. Geologists use the word to define a special type of hill, one that formed beneath a glacier and was sculpted by the passage of the ice. New York State is something of a world capital for drumlins.

Drumlins are curious landscape features. Often they are all around, but they are much easier to see on maps than in the field. For example, the land lying north of Route 20 between Sharon Springs and Sloansville (figure 26-1) is a mix of agriculture, woodlot, and a relatively large amount of swamp. Nothing much registers to the eye, but after one look at a topographic map, a geologist instantly sees a dense field of drumlins.

Drumlins are distinctive hills. They come in all sizes, but usually they are between a half mile and a mile long, 600 to 1,200 feet wide, and 15 to 150 feet tall. A drumlin is elliptical, shaped like an upside-down spoon bowl stretched out with the

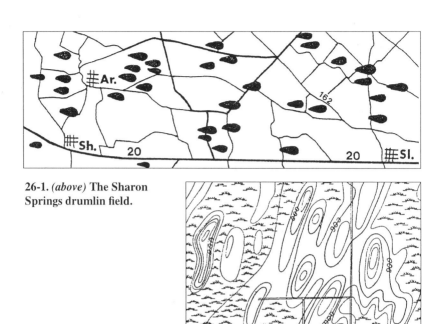

26-1. *(above)* The Sharon Springs drumlin field.

26-2. *(right)* Geometry of drumlins.

widest dimension near the upstream end, the rest tapering off downstream (figure 26-2).

It's not known exactly how drumlins form, because what goes on at the bottom of a moving glacier is not observable. But from what we see, we can deduce that there are two mechanisms. First, moving glaciers can sculpt drumlins from pre-existing sediment by overriding older moraines. Second, glaciers can deposit drumlins directly. Glaciers carry with them a great deal of very wet, clay-rich sediment. If a glacier overruns an obstruction, there is a tendency for the wet sediment to compact and stabilize on the spot. In other words, a heap of sediment accumulates as a big lump beneath the glacier. The advancing glacier overrides that lump and sculpts it into a drumlin. No matter how they formed, the result is the rather attractive, sinuously curving hill we see.

26-3. The drumlins at Ames.

Drumlins are never alone; they are found in abundance stretching across the landscape in *drumlin fields*. Often there are just a few scores of drumlins in a region, but sometimes there are many more. There are 3,000 drumlins in south-central New England; there is a field of about 5,000 in Wisconsin. The greatest of all the North American drumlin fields is right here in New York State. The field begins along the southwestern shore of Lake Erie and extends eastward all the way to the southeastern corner of that lake. Our field is smaller, but still impressive—it covers most of the southern flank of the Mohawk Valley. In all, there are about 10,000 drumlins in New York State.

The eastern end of the Mohawk field lies just north of the Catskills. It begins near Duanesburg and stretches off to the west; Route 20 runs along the southern edge of the field. If you drive around the back roads of this region, you'll soon notice the pronounced east-west lineation to all of the hills. If you drive north or south, you find yourself constantly going up and down slopes. These are the drumlins, and once you know what to look for, you begin to see them everywhere. Two very good ones can be seen as you approach the village of Ames from the south on Route 10. The two of them, side-by-side, are just west of town (figure 26-3).

There are more drumlins south of Route 20, especially along County Route 145 toward Cobleskill. In fact, nearly all of the hills along this road probably are drumlins. (A very impressive location of glacial sculpting is the stretch of road immediately east of Argusville. Here, the passing glaciers have created a whole host of beautiful, sinuous, east-west grooves. These are not drumlins, but are a related feature called glacial *flutes*.)

The Mohawk drumlin field formed during one of the very last readvances of glaciers into the Catskill vicinity. This was the Mohawk Lobe of the Laurentide glacier that penetrated westward up the Mohawk Valley about 14,000 years ago (see figure 3-2). This is the advance that reached to south of Cooperstown. There must have been plenty of sediment available to this glacier, and there may have been several older moraines lying in the way of the glacier's advance. The sediment of these old moraines probably was mobilized beneath the advancing sheet of ice and then sculpted into drumlins.

It's easy to imagine these closing times of glaciation. The Mohawk Lobe became what is called a "wet glacier" toward the end of the Wisconsin glaciation as the climate became warmer. The bottom of the glacier was much like a very wet basement, and it gurgled with the sounds of water flowing through the many crevasses within the ice. The gurgles were mixed with the steadier roar from the continuous flow of subglacial streams.

The western Mohawk glacier was dying. Its front was in headlong retreat. Behind the front, holes in the ice were appearing. There was a litter of boulders among desolate brown gravels. As the water drained away, the whole expanse of the landscape closely matched the dry valleys of today's Antarctica. But this would not last for long. Here and there, green patches began to appear.

27

The Legacy

THE CATSKILLS OF TODAY are a legacy handed down from the glacial times of long ago. The landscape generates fabulous images of glaciation that haunt these mountains. These images make vivid impressions upon me wherever I go: From the escarpment trail above the Hudson Valley, I can see the huge streams of ice that filled and traveled southward through that valley several times. When I climb Slide Mountain, I can visualize the white currents that once lapped against its summit; I watch the flow of ice separate, and then pass around that mountaintop like a parting current of water. As I travel the Schoharie, Delaware or Susquehanna Rivers, I see the smaller glaciers that once pushed their way down these valleys. I cannot pass between the slopes of Grand Gorge Gap without feeling the presence of torrents of the swollen and agitated whitewater stream that once passed though this gap in the mountains. To the north, I can see the great melting glacier that fed these cataracts. Then there are the glacial lakes—I cannot gaze out across Schoharie Creek without seeing it filled with a deep, ice-covered lake.

There is the economic legacy. Glaciers have had an enormous and direct influence upon the economy that developed here. Virtually all of our Catskill villages are built where they are because glaciers made some of the land habitable and left other land uninhabitable. It is the same for our roads, which are often perched upon terraces of glacial gravels where the ice had already prepared a road bed. These same deposits give us our sand and gravel industry. Our agricultural flatlands lie mostly upon the floors of old glacial lakes. But the biggest economic legacy is our scenic domain. Much of our recreational hiking and climbing is upon scenery carved by the passing ice.

Glaciers have greatly influenced the cultural heritage we have developed here in the Catskills, as well. Catskill history, art, and literature are all set in a landscape sculpted by the passage of glaciers. Almost all of our cultural heritage passed through the doors of the Catskill Mountain House. The old hotel probably was the single most important enterprise ever established in these mountains. It strongly and directly influenced the development of American arts and literature, and as such, it is central to the region's, if not the nation's, cultural history.

But the complex ebb and flow of the hotel's history is interwoven with the long-ago passage of glaciers: The hotel was perched upon a glacially-carved ledge overlooking a glacially-carved valley. The lakes behind the hotel occupied glacially-scoured basins. The peaks that surrounded the hotel were sculpted by the great glaciers that once passed here. The kind of appreciation for nature that we take for granted today was novel one hundred years ago. Thomas Cole nurtured this appreciation, and when it matured, the forest preserves of the Catskills and the Adirondacks were the most obvious results. All of this preceded and foretold much about the environmental ethics of our own time.

Glaciers do not in themselves produce art, literature, or environmental ethics, but they can create a setting which can inspire all three. That is quite a legacy.

June 10, 1994 AD

I was driving with Sam Adams to the top of Peekamoose Gorge. At the top, Sam told me where to pull over. He quickly climbed down onto a streambank along the south side of the road. After poking around for a while, he found what he was looking for and motioned me to stick my arm into a hole in the ground. I was a little cautious at first, but then I realized what was down there. The air of the hole was frigid on this warm summer day. It was an ice cave. My arm couldn't reach any of the ice, but it was down there. I pondered the ice cave for a moment. "All that's left," I thought.

Important References

Atwood, W. *The Physiographic Provinces of North America.* Boston: Ginn and Co., 1940.

Bierhorst, John. *The Ashokan Catskills: A Natural History.* The Catskill Center for Conservation and Development and Fleischmanns, N.Y.: Purple Mountain Press, 1995.

Cadwell, Donald H. "Late Wisconsinan Stratigraphy of the Catskill Mountains," in Donald H. Cadwell, ed., *The Wisconsinan Stage of the First Geological District, Eastern New York.* Albany: New York State Museum Bulletin 455, 1986.

Chamberlain, R. and R. Sallisbury. *College Geology, Part I: Processes.* New York: Henry Holt, 1927.

Dawson, Alistair. *Ice Age Earth.* New York: Routledge, 1992.

Dineen, Robert J. "Deglaciation of the Hudson Valley Between Hyde Park and Albany, New York," in Donald H. Cadwell, ed., *The Wisconsinan Stage of the First Geological District, Eastern New York.* Albany: New York State Museum, Bulletin No. 455, 1986.

Evers, Alf. T*he Catskills: From Wilderness to Woodstock.* Woodstock, NY: Overlook Press, 1982.

Fleisher, Jay. "Glacial Morphology of upper Susquehanna Drainage," in P.C. Wilson, ed., *Guidebook to Field Excursions.* New York State Geological Association Annual Meeting, 1977.

___. *Glacial Geology and Late Wisconsinan Stratigraphy, Upper Susquehanna Drainage Basin, New York.* New York State Museum, Bulletin No. 455, 1986.

___. "Active and Stagnant Ice Retreat: Deglaciation of Central New York State," in J. Ebert, *New York State Geological Association Field Trip Guidebook,* 1991.

Flint, Richard Foster. *Glacial and Quaternary Geology.* New York: John Wiley and Sons, 1971.

Isachsen, Y.W., et al. *Geology of New York: A Simplified Account.* Albany: New York State Museum, Educational Leaflet No. 28, 1991.

Kelly, Franklin, et al. *Frederic Edwin Church.* Washington, D.C.: Smithsonian Press, 1990.

Rich, John Lyon. *Glacial Geology of the Catskills.* Albany: New York State Museum Bulletin No. 299, 1935.

Van Zandt, Roland. *The Catskill Mountain House.* New Brunswick, N.J.:Rutgers University Press, 1966.

The Author

Like many paleontologists, Robert Titus began hunting for fossils as a young child. His fascination with fossils and rocks eventually led to his career as a geologist. He was drawn to upstate New York by the area's natural beauty and he has taught at Hartwick College since 1974. Titus began a second career as a writer in 1991, when he began a regular column for *Kaatskill Life* magazine. He is the author of *The Catskills: A Geological Guide*, also published by Purple Mountain Press.